You Herd Me!

I'll Say It If Nobody Else Will

You Herd Me!
Colin Cowherd

THREE RIVERS PRESS
NEW YORK

THREE RIVERS PRESS and the Tugboat design are
registered trademarks of Random House LLC.

Originally published in hardcover in the United States by
Crown Archetype, an imprint of the Crown Publishing Group,
a division of Random House LLC, New York, in 2013.

Library of Congress Cataloging-in-Publication Data
Cowherd, Colin.
    You herd me! : I'll say it if nobody else will / Colin Cowherd.
        p.   cm.
    1. Cowherd, Colin. 2. Sportscasters—United States—
Biography. 3. Sports & Recreation—Essays. 4. Humor—
Topic—Sports. 5. Biography & Autobiography—Sports.
GV742.42.C69 A3   2013
070.449796092   [B]
2013032217

ISBN 978-0-8041-3813-0
eBook ISBN 978-0-8041-3790-4

Printed in the United States of America

Cover design by Michael Nagin
Cover photograph: Deborah Feingold

10 9 8 7 6 5 4 3 2 1

First Paperback Edition

For my parents, Charles and Patricia,
who gave me the curiosity to write what you are about to read

Contents

Introduction

We were running late to the game, which probably didn't mean as much to my dad as it did to me. He was a workaholic who was chronically behind schedule, so this was nothing out of the ordinary for either one of us. Besides, this wasn't *his* first live sporting event, only mine. And so it was *my* heart that sank when we arrived at the parking lot at the high school gym in Hoquiam, Washington, and found nearly every spot taken. From the passenger seat of my dad's Buick Riviera, I looked out the window and imagined every spot inside the gym was taken as well.

Of course it was packed. It could be no other way. Within those walls were the great Harlem Globetrotters, the ones I'd seen on *Wide World of Sports* a couple of months earlier. Who *wouldn't* want to be there?

The Riviera added to our problems. It wouldn't fit into any of the smaller parking spaces, so our late arrival to the lot was merely the beginning. As we wound our way in and out of the parking lanes, unable to find a spot big enough to dock Dad's boat, I could feel the minutes pass. Seconds late became minutes late. As my dad made a sharp turn into an alley behind the gym, the way I viewed sports changed forever.

There, right in front of us, was the Globetrotters' bus. We were face to face, squared off like mismatched fighters, the Riviera and the grille of the parked bus. A pair of players leaning on the bus suddenly stood up straight when they saw us.

And that was the moment my view of sports changed forever.

My eyes went to something shiny in one of their hands. It was a can of beer. As a kid who approached sports with the innocence of a Clair Bee novel, where every athlete was a hero on and off the field, forever capable of hitting a home run for a sick boy in the hospital, I felt like I'd been punched in the gut. They were sharing a cold one right before "Sweet Georgia Brown." How could that be? This wasn't the way it worked. My mind reeled. It was a Miller, although I have no idea why I remember that or why it ever seemed important to the eight-year-old me.

Both 'Trotters looked straight through our windshield and directly into my eyes. I had caught them, and they caught me catching them. My innocence was swallowed along with the last swig of the champagne of beers. They weren't smiling like they did on television. There were no friendly laughs or buckets of confetti. They glared at my dad and me with a look that said, "You shouldn't be here, and if you say anything, you'll regret it."

My dad quickly slammed the Riviera into reverse, backed out, and eventually found a parking space. We didn't talk about what we saw. He was probably as disgusted as I was mystified.

First impressions have a powerful influence over an eight-year-old. Seeds are planted and grow from there, often wildly out of control. Tiny shards of truth come together to create an experience that makes the world look like it's being viewed in a funhouse mirror.

That moment in the parking lot lasted only seconds, but the impression it created is still imprinted deep in my emotional archive.

The alley.
The beer.
The stares.

I guarantee you one thing: What the rest of the crowd saw that night in the cramped gym in Hoquiam wasn't what I saw. They saw a show. I saw the truth.

The game itself held no virtue. My hometown was so small,

we probably didn't even get the real Globetrotters. It was something that resembled the Globetrotters on discount, an outlet-store version of the real thing. Maybe the East Harlem Globetrotters. Meadowlark Lemon wasn't on the floor, that's for sure, and I recall the shooting percentage being far lower that night than it ever was on my television. They quit taking half-court hook shots before they made one.

Still, it was basketball with confetti and a ladder, and that has a strange appeal to a kid. I watched and probably laughed a few times, but I made sure never to make eye contact with the players I saw standing next to the bus.

My Globetrotter experience didn't reshape my views on sports—it created them. I had no previous experience to measure it against, so it stuck. It's still there to this day.

The unvarnished truth is the only kind I know. Brutal honesty is the only option.

There's got to be another angle. Don't believe the press release. It's all being shaped for our consumption.

Most important, form your own opinion.

A few years after the Globetrotter incident, my best friend's brother, Brad Jones, was invited into the Oakland Raiders' locker room. His most lasting impression wasn't the size of Art Shell's arms or the shininess of Otis Sistrunk's bald head. Instead, I sat listening with rapt attention as Brad breathlessly relayed the story of watching quarterback Kenny Stabler and receiver Fred Biletnikoff, both Pro Bowlers, playing cards in their jockstraps. He may have said they were smoking, too, but maybe that's just a detail I created to embellish the scene. Either way, this was yet another glimpse backstage into the grimier side of athletics. As it turned out, the sports world wasn't one long after-school special playing on an endless loop. It was a flawed world inhabited by flawed humans who did shocking things like drink beer before a game and play cards in their jockstraps.

There are really two games: the one you see and the one you don't. The way I see it, the best way to use access to both worlds is to illuminate and reveal, not idolize and adore.

It's better to be wrong than to be played for a fool.

Sometimes I wonder, is my mind playing tricks on me? The brain will do that, you know. First impressions become distorted over time. Memories can be unreliable. My childhood was filled with divorces and uncertainty, but sports were a constant. I had a lonely upbringing. My sister ignored me; five years older, she understandably didn't want to hang out with a hyperactive little brother. My father, an optometrist, was, like most men of his generation, an emotionally distant workaholic.

Games and standings and statistics were my constant companions, bringing solidity to the fluidity of my life. They were always there for me, baseball in the summer, football in the fall, basketball in the winter. I sought attention, and knowing the backstage stories—the beer-drinking 'Trotters and card-playing Raiders— meant access and a measure of popularity for a kid growing up largely ignored in a small, rural community.

Those were the stories I wanted to tell then. They're the stories I want to tell now.

The backstage stories helped to shape my worldview. I knew stuff that nobody else did, and I liked the feeling. I lived in the rainiest corner of the country, but when I think back to my childhood my mind recalls only a string of sunny days. There are no dark clouds in my memory, which has to mean something, doesn't it? Is it a metaphor for the path my life would eventually take? A defense mechanism? Who really knows?

My first eye-opening sports experience was real, though.

The alley.
The beer.
The stares.
Hell yes, it was real.
And hell yes, it changed everything.

Two things make smart men stupid. Beautiful women and sports.

Addiction or Fiction?

Eight large glasses of water a day. Remember that? To be a healthy human being, you needed to drink eight large glasses of water a day. This was a fact, no debate allowed. Doctors, school nurses, anybody with a stethoscope—even a toy stethoscope—stated it as a matter of biblical certainty.

Even as a kid, I knew this was bullshit. The Surgeon General could have stopped by my house with the yellowed food pyramid chart from the wall of my junior high and I still wouldn't have believed him.

Eight large glasses of water a day. Who lives like that, a dolphin? Two large glasses of water at every meal and you're still coming up far short. Are we supposed to bring a garden hose to work?

Where's Colin?

He's in the bathroom, where he has spent the majority of his life.

Years after this was accepted as fact, a report by the *British Medical Journal,* backed by the *American Journal of Physiology,* walked back the ironclad truth of eight glasses a day. It found that liquid, not water, was the important part of the equation. A cup of coffee counts. An apple counts. A baked potato, 75 percent water, counts as much as a glass of water.

So the eight-glasses-a-day thing wasn't really true. And neither was the hype over a high-fiber diet. Decades after that craze, we were told that excessive fiber could reduce your life span. As a kid whose mother forced him to eat Raisin Bran every morning, I was hoping they'd come to that conclusion far earlier.

My point is this: you don't have to be an expert to know that some things don't make sense.

The water thing never rang true to me.

Neither did the idea that Tiger Woods was a sex addict.

After twenty-four years of covering sports, too many aspects of the Tiger-as-addict story failed to ring true. The nonsports media swarmed on this story and showed their ignorance of the sports world and the modern athlete every step of the way. They helped to legitimize the idea that Tiger was "suffering" from a disease, that he had no control over his actions, and that he should, in fact, be viewed with pity and not scorn.

Oh, please.

Can someone bring me another glass of water? I think I'm a glass short today.

Tiger's fall from grace began when he wrecked his SUV outside his mansion in Florida. From there we learned that he was an inveterate skirt-chaser who ran around on his wife and screwed everyone from Vegas party girls to the waitress at the local coffee shop.

This, of course, presented a public-relations problem for Tiger. Sordid details about his life were splashed everywhere. Sponsors dropped him almost as fast as his wife, Elin Nordegren, did. In an instant, his image was changed forever.

What did Tiger become in the public eye? Deceitful, unfeeling, misogynistic.

There wasn't much to say in Tiger's defense. Every news story made him sound worse. Women came forward like an advancing army, each one willing to tell her story for a price.

How would Tiger get rehabilitated in the public eye? How could he transform the public image of the unfeeling horndog back into something resembling the endorsement machine who entered every tournament as a heavy favorite? Only one way: by becoming a victim. And who could possibly accomplish that feat?

Who could turn America's most notorious cad into a sympathetic figure?

Nike, of course.

He lost all his major endorsements. Except one.

Nike.

And *how* could this happen?

Only one way:

Tiger had to go from villain to victim.

What was he if he *wasn't* a bad person who did terrible things to the people closest to him?

He was a sex addict.

He couldn't help himself.

The whole sex thing was out of his control. He wasn't a guy who just wanted to use his clout as the most powerful athlete in the world by having sex with as many women as he could. No way—he was a *sex addict* whose life was consumed by his compulsion.

So off he went to the rehab clinic, where he would undergo intensive therapy intended to cure him of his addiction to having sex with beautiful women who weren't his wife. He would be sequestered out of the public eye, free to work on his debilitating disease and come to terms with his behavior in private.

And while he was in there, I certainly hope he had his eight glasses of water a day.

Sex addict. Give me a break.

First, sexual addiction is not even a medically accepted diagnosis. You could look it up—I did. The controversy surrounding the mere existence of this "disease" devalues any fact-based contention that Tiger was, in fact, an addict.

But let's go ahead and play along. (After all, that's exactly what the nonsports media world did.) Let's assume for the sake of argument that sexual addiction is real, and Tiger Woods—the most famous and richest athlete in the world—was afflicted with it.

Sexual addiction, by its very nature, is defined as being so intense and compulsive, it derails your life. It's an addiction, so it's difficult for anything else to intrude on the act of feeding the addiction. And yet, from the time Tiger Woods was married (October 2004) to the day of the SUV incident that exposed his infidelity and led to his diagnosis, he won six majors and twenty-five events.

Does that sound like someone whose life was irretrievably disrupted? Does that sound like someone who couldn't focus on any other aspect of life but the addiction?

The truth is, he was never better than when he was in the throes of this debilitating, paralyzing disease.

And you know when Tiger *stopped* winning? When he went into sex rehab.

The only reason his addiction became an issue is because his wife found out. It wasn't because it was interfering so greatly with his life that he couldn't putt or hit a fairway. The first sign of addiction was his wife finding a text message.

Second, Woods clearly had something to gain by entering a sexual-addiction clinic: his image. At this point, his career was being handled almost exclusively by the brilliant marketing minds at Nike. As other sponsors bailed, Nike not only hung on but took control of his flailing career to craft a shrewd recovery plan.

You can almost see them sitting around a big table in a big boardroom and one of them saying, "We're in the brand-building business, and we're going to save him."

Addicts are sympathetic. They're at the mercy of their addiction, so how can they be villains?

Third, it's an acknowledged fact that rich, famous, athletic men get much more sex—and get it far easier—than the rest of us. Woods wasn't the local mailman or traveling salesman, having to work overtime and concoct crazy stories to get his fix. He wasn't even the run-of-the-mill celebrity—the kind Dr. Drew helps in his Pasadena, California, rehab center. No, he was a one-man conglomerate, the world's most recognizable athlete, a guy who made $40 million a year from endorsements alone.

Tiger Freaking Woods.

He had dozens of people at his disposal, all eager to curry favor by doing El Tigre's dirty work. He could make one phone call and set up any sexual encounter he could imagine—and that's exactly what he reportedly did.

According to media reports, Tiger had fifteen affairs in five years of marriage.

Now, I don't want to sound flippant here, and I'm not trying to get anyone in trouble, but in my experience covering sports, that number is a low one for most star athletes, married or not. Framing Woods as some out-of-control, wild-eyed sexual monster doesn't ring true.

You know what he sounds like? The backup small forward for every NBA team.

Tiger wasn't a sex addict. He was simply a virile young man in a hollow marriage. He plays a sport with a lot of downtime, and he was looking for hookups.

That's not an addiction.

Regrettably, it's too often just the life of an American professional athlete.

We have to understand the unique place professional athletes hold in the culture. They're often compared to actors, but the median salary for an actor in America is $39,500 a year. Not every actor is George Clooney. Corporate CEOs might be rich, but they're usually 60 years old. Politicians might be powerful, but most of them are older and not always attractive.

Professional athletes have everything: youth, wealth, looks, power. And they have the added bonus of travel, which allows them the sexual freedom no other industry can offer.

Over the past couple of decades, professional athletes have made giant leaps, right over the heads of not only regular citizens but also the swankiest celebrities. Compare that sub-$40,000 actor's median to the median salary of the NFL's 1,800 players: $770,000.

And these numbers are strictly salaries. It doesn't take into account endorsements, which are often larger than the actual salaries for players, especially in sports such as tennis, golf, and the NBA.

Tiger Woods was not just *some* jock. He wasn't some median-salary PGA pro hoping to break into the top ten at the Tucson Open. He was *the* jock, perhaps the world's most recognizable human behind the pope and President Obama.

My point is this: you can't take the concept of sexual addiction as it may apply to 90 percent of the world and apply it to Tiger Woods. Call him what you will—unfaithful, deceitful, uncaring—but please don't say that his decision to have multiple sex partners works the same way it would with the rest of us.

Remember back to when the story broke and Tiger went into rehab. He not only exited the public stage—he disappeared. He went into such deep seclusion nobody could even get a photo of him. In this age of iPhones and sports blogs and paparazzi and TMZ, when a lot of people would have paid a lot of money for a quick shot of Woods, it was more than a week later when a fuzzy shot of a guy who looked like Tiger—wearing a hoodie and standing on the porch of a condo-looking place we assume was the rehab center—was published on Radar online.

More than a week. Who can hide for more than a week? Not even the biggest actor can hide for more than a week.

Tiger Woods can hide for more than a week.

That's power. That's exclusivity. That's juice.

The sports world is different, and Woods was different within that world. He was a one-man subcategory of a small subcategory. Athletes understand this. During the 2010 Winter Olympics, *Time* magazine's Sean Gregory interviewed an athlete on the morning of Tiger's famous sex-addict press conference. This athlete, told that Woods hugged a few people after stepping down from the podium, joked about Tiger's so-called addiction and said of the people he hugged, "They're like, 'Yeah, you're awesome. You go have that sex.'"

That athlete? Lindsey Vonn, who ended up becoming Tiger's first public relationship in the postaddict phase of his life. It's interesting that Vonn was married at the time of Tiger's fall, too. Even she laughed at him. Her words reflected the general feeling among athletes and people who understand the sports world.

It was a staged apology for a staged problem.

But I'm sure I speak for everyone when I say I'm just hoping and praying Tiger has been cured of his addiction. I think there's some evidence that his rehabilitation was successful. The biggest indication came in March of 2012. That's when Tiger won the Bay Hill tournament, his first win since the sex scandal of 2009.

Sex addict.

Please.

Someone get me a glass of water.

Fans want to hold me to sports opinions from a month or a year ago. Yet, what if new information comes to light? You wouldn't want your doctor or stockbroker using outdated information or science. Why should I?

Torn in the USA

've traveled to forty-seven or forty-eight states, settling in only five, and I'm here to tell you there's a stark difference between visiting a place and sinking some roots, no matter how deep. A home, a lawn, a neighbor—*that's* how you get to know the heart of a place.

From a safe distance, maybe while vacationing from the North during another long winter, Tampa probably feels like a reasonably priced Valhalla. It's got everything you'd want for a quick escape: cheap golf, warm weather, quiet beaches. It's an affordable paradise.

From a distance.

The twenty months I spent living in Tampa felt like twenty years. To me, the draining heat and humidity from May through October made it feel like Libya with an NFL franchise. Or maybe Kenya with a Ruby Tuesday's. It was crowded with retirees who moved there, drove slowly, complained too much, registered to vote in order to vote No on virtually everything.

School bonds? No.

Infrastructure improvements? No.

A new park? Hell, no.

I had a running joke with friends who wanted to visit: fly into Atlanta and follow the Waffle Houses south. After living in Las Vegas, Tampa had all the energy of a dying car battery.

And yet, when I returned there to cover Super Bowl XXXVII, it was a week of less-blistering sun, a lively Eagles concert with friends, and the best key lime pie this side of any other place that serves key lime pie.

Same city, two vastly different experiences.

For someone like me, who has called several places home, it was also instructive: you have to unpack your bags to truly understand a region or place. Some women you date, some you marry. But only one experience unveils a deeper truth, whatever truth that may be.

I've lived in all four corners of the country, from the Pacific Northwest to the Desert Southwest to Florida to Connecticut. The experience has given me a perspective on geography and demographics that I wouldn't have otherwise. Embedding yourself in a community, understanding what makes the residents tick and ticks them off, can be powerful.

In a roundabout way, my experiences observing people and places in all corners of the country have led me to a conclusion: sports is the Great Equalizer, maybe the fairest aspect of American life.

I don't mean to go all Toby Keith on you. You know, "Wave the flag, jump in the Ford, grab that gun, ready, aim—pew, pew, pew. God Bless 'Merica." But I will say the idea of sports in this country almost brings a salty discharge to the corner of my left eye.

When it comes to sports, this is a great country.

Politics can be a harsh and humbling reminder of our limited patch of dirt. A conservative in California or a liberal in Texas may feel his vote is worthless. The electoral system gives us a set of standings that never change; certain states are like the Astros: always hovering somewhere near last place. A lack of population often translates to a lack of funding, which can leave one-stoplight towns looking up with envy and some bitterness at the more connected and powerful.

Sports is different. Sports is our true democracy, giving everyone a sense that they can win.

High school sports, especially football and baseball, are mostly dominated by smaller towns or suburbs. Hoover, Alabama; River Ridge, Louisiana; Katy, Texas—they each have the focus, commitment, and amount of football talent that a major metro program in a place like New York City or Boston can't rival. Of 2012's top ten high school football powerhouses, as ranked by *USA Today*, eight were in towns so small their zip codes might as well have four numbers.

People who live for high school football in those towns don't envy the big cities. In fact, many may pity them. They don't coddle and worship star athletes after they've made it big; they create them.

We see the same phenomenon in college sports. They're dominated primarily by relatively small cities, such as Ann Arbor, Michigan, and Lexington, Kentucky. Tuscaloosa, Norman, College Station. They can create sustainable and profitable programs that urban universities can never duplicate. The smaller places, where it means more, have a passion that translates into funding. They travel more fans and boosters to road games than city schools have enrolled in classes.

And the media has created a world that is more condensed and less disparate. Message boards, blogs, and YouTube highlights have created connections that were unavailable decades ago. The Internet has created an endless stream of year-round recruiting information. The games might end in January for a Buckeye or Longhorn fan, but the flow of information never ends. Who needs pro sports? This is the life.

We've come to assume that professional sports is one big trophy case for the richer and more glamorous cities, but even that assumption needs to be reconsidered. Even in the pay-for-play world, the frugal, grounded, and even downright small are well represented. The Green Bay Packers have thirteen NFL championships; the New York Jets, one. The Washington Redskins sleep on piles of money and yet the Indianapolis Colts win actual playoff games. The Philadelphia 76ers have spent decades as a perpetually broken-down clunker while the Oklahoma City Thunder are perennial title contenders who could sell considerably more tickets if only they were available.

And what makes that high school football trophy that resides in River Ridge every bit as prestigious as all those Stanley Cups in Detroit is the mentality of the people in those respective cities. Do you really think anybody in Odessa, Texas, loses sleep every time the Celtics raise a banner? Do you think folks in Athens, Georgia, feel less significant just because Tom Coughlin has added a second Super Bowl win to his coaching legacy? Of course not.

All politics is local. All sports is, too, because deeply ingrained in these smaller towns is a sense that they are winning something that is every bit as important. They may wake up angry with the election of a new POTUS or feel slighted over the congressional veto of a farm subsidy, but sports gives them a sense of fulfillment and pride.

Big cities have nothing on us. We don't like their teams and don't need their pampered stars. We've got all we want right here.

Sure, fans in the Midwest feel the coasts get a disproportionately larger share of the media attention, and they're probably right. The coasts are where the masses live, and giant media conglomerates need viewers. But ask yourself this question: Would you rather be the St. Louis Cardinals, an envied baseball machine with an incredible fan base, or the New York Mets, a franchise so lacking in redeemable history that it hung wild-card banners at old Shea Stadium? Would you rather be the Packers or the remarkably well-funded and glitzy Dallas Cowboys, who have had as much playoff success over the past fifteen years as the *National Enquirer* has had on Pulitzer Prize day?

Popular can feel awfully hollow when it's sitting side-by-side with *successful*.

There's no doubt my professional travels, bouncing from one corner of the country to the next, have limited the depth of the roots I've sunk in any one town. But it's also granted me the opportunity to see things and meet people I otherwise wouldn't. It's allowed me to experience firsthand the depth of small-town loyalty that's rarely found in major cities with transient populations and athletes seeking the next monstrous free-agent deal.

Those people in smaller and more intimate places have opened my eyes to a wonderful landscape that is far too often underreported and undervalued. From white-water rafting down the Rogue River with Oregon State football fans to tailgating with Florida Gator football fans fresh off a win over rival Tennessee, I've discovered that these people don't sound or act like people who are missing out.

In a country that keeps score too often, that ranks everything we do, that pits you against me and compares everyone to everyone else, we all win with sports.

What do we want out of life? For most people, the answer starts with three simple words: *a fair shot*. Our search for *fairness* has become a mini-obsession. So, with everything from jobs to college admission supposedly politicized, where do we find this elusive concept of fairness?

Easy: you find it in sports, that's where—in every corner of this great country.

Hating an athlete for being arrogant is like hating a bat for being nocturnal.

Conservative Backlash

've always had a tough time figuring out the difference between a model and a supermodel. Is it about the cheekbones or the checkbook? The fashion or the fortune?

And where does it go from there? Once we reach critical mass on supermodels, once it becomes standard to be super, will there be a supermodel so transcendent she becomes the first super-duper-model?

Janice Dickinson claims to be the first supermodel. Since most of her success came in the 1970s and '80s, most of the world knows her primarily as just another crazy and failed reality-show has-been. Her descent has taken a predictable path: she recently filed for bankruptcy, and it's shocking—*shocking,* I say—to learn that much of her debt was to plastic surgeons and folks known as "cosmetic-procedure professionals."

Remember, this woman started out gorgeous. From birth she was painted by a brush wielded by nature's most skilled artist. Yet her desperation to look young has left her broke, pathetic, and overly Botoxed.

Dickinson's not alone, of course. Most people want to remain as attractive as possible for as long as possible. Nobody wants to surrender to age, but where do you draw the line? When do those tight jeans on the fit 46-year-old mom devolve into the realm of *she's trying way too hard*? When does the Affliction T-shirt on the slightly overweight middle-aged guy take the fateful turn from *hey, trendy* to *obviously recently divorced*?

The line between *aging gracefully* and *you're too old to be wearing that* is razor-thin. Which side of the line you occupy can be determined by something as random as a momentary lapse of judgment at a retailer.

By the same token, there's an argument to be made for making every effort to keep up with the times. As pathetic as people might look in their never-ending quest to retain their youth, they still get points for trying, right? It's the folks who ignore or reject change—whether technological or otherwise—who are the ones being left behind.

And that's why two major American institutions—Major League Baseball and the Republican Party—could use an Ed Hardy T-shirt, a little collagen in the lips, a nip here and a tuck there.

Both are well funded and entrenched, and neither is eager to admit either weakness or defeat. They share a troubling trend of doubling down on ideas that have proven to be unpopular rather than adapting to broaden their appeal. Both are undeniably ex-heavyweights who have been knocked down a peg or two by younger, more connected, and more progressive rivals.

For baseball, the rival is the NFL; for the GOP, it's the Democratic Party. The NFL and the Democrats seem to subscribe to an inclusive theory while MLB and the GOP are hidebound and determined to remain loyal to their core followers—*The Base,* in politispeak. As a result, they often appear outdated and rigid.

Liberals and football zealots shouldn't get too excited by the recent trend, though: neither MLB or the GOP is going away anytime soon.

In 2012, the Republicans put forward a presidential candidate who looked like the publisher of *Yachting Weekly,* who made a late, major campaign gaffe, and whose own son described him by saying, "Nobody has ever wanted to be president less than my dad."

Despite all that, Mitt Romney captured 47 percent of the popular vote. His relative success was a sign that there are plenty of sizable groups, businesses, and states that lean strongly right. From Wall Streeters, to large swaths of the Midwest, to most of the South, to married women, to men over 60, to rural America, the GOP's core message—regardless of candidate—still resonates. Romney's ability to raise nearly $1 billion for his campaign is evidence enough.

Similarly, MLB stands on its own merits. More than 75 million tickets were sold during the 2012 season, and there are several envious hot spots—San Francisco, St. Louis, Boston—where baseball passions run high. Like the GOP, money is not a problem for baseball; lucrative new television contracts with ESPN, Fox, and Turner are worth more than $1 billion. Local teams like the Dodgers ($260 million annually) have monster television deals in their home markets.

That $260 million is just one revenue source for one team.

Damn. Holla at your Hanley Ramirez.

The GOP and MLB: similar qualities, similar problems.

In a broad sense, they just can't manage to keep up with the times. The NFL has a good grasp on the shortened attention spans and competing interests of young viewers. It created the Red Zone Channel to condense the game to its most important elements and give fans the illusion of nonstop scoring—perfect for fantasy leaguers and gamblers alike. The NFL has also added broadcast features like the electronic first-down line, one of those innovations—like cell phones—we can't imagine doing without. Just about every year the NFL devises a new policy, rule, or media strategy—for instance, moving free agency up a few weeks to compete with March Madness—designed to keep the game fresh and in the public eye year-round.

Yet baseball . . . well, baseball tends to move at a slower pace.

Football is going faster—more more *more!*—while baseball continues to mosey its way down the road a piece, content to get wherever it's going whenever it gets there.

Baseball can't really figure out what it wants to do with instant replay, so it stays the course and allows its managers to waste time arguing on the field when it would take half the time to look at a replay and get the damned thing right. And even when it does use replay, it takes too long and doesn't always produce a satisfying result. Remember the Oakland Athletics' home run that wasn't in May of 2013? It was obvious to everyone within ten seconds of seeing a replay, but the umpires left the field and took far too long to get the call wrong.

It's a rapidly changing culture, and the NFL gets it. Baseball is still waxing philosophical about its hallowed records and calling it entertainment when people dressed as sausages and dead presidents run around the field. It's institutional stagnation.

Not surprisingly given the reluctance to embrace technology and new ideas, baseball's demographics skew to the elderly side. Its audience, much like the GOP's, is getting really old. A deep dig into the ratings for the 2012 NLDS reveals that young men would rather pay to watch an MMA event than get free playoff baseball. That should be an eye-opener throughout Bud Selig's Park Avenue office.

This same inability to connect has hampered the conservative party in recent presidential elections. After Romney's drubbing, the Fox News narrative—led by Sean Hannity—changed overnight. Polling illustrated just how thoroughly Latino voters rejected the GOP platform, so Hannity suddenly claimed he had "evolved"—the very next night, he could see a pathway to citizenship for all current Americans. Wow. Talk about a quick-change artist. And longtime GOP strategist and operative Karl Rove, who so profoundly misjudged the election for months, was off the air faster than Howard Stern's replacements.

Until just recently, it's probable that Hannity and Rove considered "social media" taking a columnist to lunch.

Stagnation leads to arrogance, which leads to insularity, which leads to fear, which leads to a lack of progress. More money equals bigger walls and bigger houses and less interaction. The GOP and MLB are both suffering from an arrogance that manifests itself through an inability to reach out to those who fall just outside the comfort zone. For baseball, it's the African-American community; for the GOP, it's any minority you can name.

To put it bluntly, both institutions have become old and white in a world that is becoming less of both.

I can make the case that a list of the GOP's current maladies mirror—almost eerily—the same issues facing Major League Baseball:

1. A struggle to attract minority participation
2. Loss of ground to their primary rival on digital and technological connectivity
3. Inflexibility
4. Appearance of a "Good Ol' Boys" club
5. Loss of the youth vote
6. Lack of new and energizing leadership

This is not a blanket condemnation of both institutions. The GOP shouldn't disregard its core financial principles and all of its social beliefs to chase alienated voters. By the same token, MLB shouldn't alter the essence of its traditions and beliefs. Both entities are fully capable of rebounding with an influx of fresh ideas and progressive leadership.

The overriding message, however, is clear: wealth, tradition, and historical relevance do not guarantee never-ending success. Sometimes hidebound institutions need to understand that reaching out, taking risks, embracing new technology, and engaging new communities is not selling your soul.

Evolving is not conceding. It's not a desperate act or a refutation of values or a bow-down to a passing fad.

The GOP and MLB think the path to cool lies in that Affliction T-shirt. When the occasion permits, they grab it out of the drawer, pull it over their heads, and strain to tug it down over their potbellies. They swagger into a club, just a couple of 60-year-olds with no self-awareness, and expect the rest of us to want to hang out.

Sorry, guys—the party's over here.

Social media: Don't do it after a cocktail or in your underwear.

The Cult of (Bad) Personality

There was billowing smoke, fresh skid marks, and debris scattered across the highway. A fender and a door panel were tossed halfway across the lane, and an ambulance siren could be heard in the distance. People were driving slowly, rubbernecking as they passed. This was almost exactly like any ugly accident; it happened suddenly, without warning, but the aftermath was bound to last forever.

The only difference? This pile-up happened on the radio.

University of Wisconsin basketball coach Bo Ryan was a guest of *Mike and Mike,* and they were discussing the relevant topic of player transfers. It's a situation coaches face regularly, and it was pertinent to the moment because Ryan was dealing with a Badger player named Jarrod Uthoff, who had expressed his desire to leave Madison for another program.

These things happen. No big deal, right? Couples break up, employees change jobs, kids leave and change schools. In college sports, of course, coaches make their names in one place and immediately jump ship to land in more glamorous and lucrative ships.

The college-recruiting process is built largely on an artificial premise. Players choose schools based on showy, manipulative weekend sales pitches. Once on campus, when faced with the reality of bad weather, 8 a.m. classes, and militaristic coaches, some of them decide they'd rather be somewhere else.

Once word spread that Ryan was blocking many of Uthoff's choices, there was bound to be tension between the coach and the radio hosts. Ryan was grumpy, which is understandable when a talented player decides to bolt. But that doesn't excuse what followed: roughly ten minutes of arrogance, delusion, defiance, and that special brand of bad public relations that made you wonder if the rest of the Badgers' athletic department—or at least the branch that could have prevented this—was suddenly deciding to take the rest of the week off.

Ryan took shots at one of the hosts for having never played the game, which apparently prevented him from understanding the issue. He inferred that multimillionaire coaches are the victims and the unpaid college players should be held to their word. He was rigid and mean when the moment seemed to call for at least a semblance of nuance and compassion.

It was radio gold for *Mike and Mike*.

It was verbal quicksand for Bo Ryan.

I'm guessing I was less surprised than most. I had not only heard that special brand of arrogance and defiance—Freud's id, ego, and superego packed into one radio segment—but I had seen it repeatedly from other members of that same group of men: college basketball coaches.

They hold a unique place in the coaching world, one filled with unsurpassed, unchallenged power that over time grows into a delusional fiefdom. They challenge university presidents and boards—their *bosses*, remember—to public verbal fistfights. Their arrogance knows no bounds.

Roy Williams once angrily dismissed a reporter, Bonnie Bernstein, on live national television, for having the audacity to ask if reports that he was leaving Kansas for North Carolina were true. Several hours later, Williams was on a private jet heading toward his new coaching destination.

Bobby Knight reportedly threw a potted plant at someone in his office over a disagreement. Jerry Tarkanian asked boosters to declare war on his school president while he was coaching at UNLV. Many of these men, like UConn's Jim Calhoun, express their on-campus omnipotence by demanding to name their replacement after their ruling power subsides.

Can you imagine another public employee believing this to-the-grave power is not only acceptable but a God-given right?

These are just the incidents we know, the few that make their way out of the almost hermetically sealed dictatorships. Behind the curtain, the Oz goes about his business in an even more power-hungry and deluded fashion.

Why? What created this culture, and what allows it to persist?

The best way to look at the phenomenon is by comparison: college basketball coach vs. college football coach.

Start with Gary Williams, the longtime coach of Maryland in the basketball-obsessed ACC. He won the 2001–2002 NCAA championship, but he finished five of the next nine years unranked. After that title, he never finished with a higher ranking than 17 in the other four. That's nine years of absolutely average basketball in the preeminent basketball conference in the country, for a school that is competing for recruits with North Carolina and Duke, not to mention Georgetown and other Big East schools. And yet he sort of slithers out of his job and into retirement. He wasn't forced out. People remember the championship year far more vividly than the nine that followed it.

The corollary to Williams is Gene Chizik at Auburn. The man won the national title and was run out of town two years later. Two years! How's that for institutional memory? Les Miles has won 85 percent of his games at LSU—85 percent!—and half the state wants to run him out of town. John Cooper averaged 9½ wins at Ohio State over his final six years, was No. 2 in the country twice over those six years, and won the Rose and the Sugar Bowls against excellent teams. And yet Cooper was run out of town because he couldn't beat Michigan. I would contend that North Carolina coach Roy Williams could lose to Duke ten straight times and still keep his job as long as the Tar Heels make the NCAA Tournament and finished in the upper third of the ACC.

What does this mean? College football coaches need either the press or public sentiment on their side. They need to at least *try* to exhibit some level of basic human decency. The only way a college football coach at a big-time school can survive a couple of bad seasons is to draw on the reserve of goodwill he's built up during the good years. Basketball is a huge revenue-producer in only a select number of schools. The money in college sports is all—all—in football. Even basketball powerhouses like Duke, Kansas, and Syracuse fire terrible football coaches because you at least have to be viable in football to make money. Yet there are several college football powers—Penn State, Georgia, USC—that seemingly ignore their basketball programs. They just hope they don't hemorrhage money. The bottom line? You can survive with a bad basketball program as long as your football program is successful.

Can the average sports fan even name Georgia's basketball coach? How about Auburn's? The schools don't care that much because the money is on the football field. And what does that mean? It means the pressure is on the football coach. He lives in constant fear of losing his job. He needs the public on his side. He needs the media on his side. Outside of Nick Saban, you can get run out at any time in college football because you need to make money and you need to win because it carries every other college sport.

Every college football coach is a season away from unemployment. They know it and they accept it. Mark Richt has won ten games in eight of his twelve years as football coach at Georgia. He's coached the team to three BCS bowl games, which is the football equivalent of the Elite Eight. He's won 75 percent of his games in the toughest conference in the country. And yet he's constantly on the verge of being fired. In fact, it's probably a miracle that he's still there.

Even at a non-SEC school, in a place with as weird a relationship with football as Berkeley, the football coach has to get results—or else. Jeff Tedford took over one of the worst programs in college football in 2002, won more games than any coach in school history, and came within one win of a spot in a national championship game in 2004. Can you imagine that: Cal in the BCS Championship game? A 23-17 loss to USC that year was the only thing that kept it from happening. Tedford rode the good-will generated from turning around the program to a $321 million renovation of Memorial Stadium and the construction of a first-class training facility. He finally got the trappings he thought he needed to compete nationally for recruits, and what happened? He got fired after he went 3-9 in 2012.

Almost every BCS school is a football school first and foremost, and the ones that aren't want to be. At a school where college basketball is important, the coach is more powerful than the athletic director. And if the coach is smart, and most of them are, he's got his formula down pat: he schedules the first ten games at home, picking the opponents to make sure he's going to win nine or ten of them; he recruits well enough to finish slightly better than .500 in conference, which ensures he's going to get a spot in the NCAA Tournament. If he can do this often enough, if he can repeat that formula, he becomes flameproof. You can't fire him. How do you fire a guy who has six straight tournament appearances? It's really, really hard.

Sometimes college basketball coaches can't even lose for losing. How's that for a great gig? When a team of exalted stature gets upset in the first round of March Madness, as Syracuse did when it lost to Vermont in 2005, it's celebrated as another example of the glory of the NCAA Tournament. Anything can happen. It's the Magic of Madness. There's an entire mythology built up over games like that, so the coach of the high seed who loses doesn't feel the same kind of heat that Nick Saban did when his heavily favored Alabama team lost to the Utah team in the 2009 Sugar Bowl. Saban was ripped for that game—he lost to Kyle Whittingham?—even though Utah ended the season as the only undefeated team in the country.

Which brings up another point: not all bowl games are created equal, and a bowl game is not equivalent to an NCAA Tournament appearance. The fourth-place finisher in the SEC West will go to a bowl game, might even *win* a bowl game, but that's not how they define a good season. The coach at Nebraska can go to the Humanitarian Bowl, but he better not make a habit of it if he wants to keep his job. Richt is twelve for twelve in bowl games at Georgia; you think anyone in Athens is impressed by that? You think they even count the Chick-fil-A, Music City, and Liberty? The only guy who does is probably Richt's agent.

On the other hand, a college basketball coach can finish fifth in the ACC, go to the tournament as a No. 8 or 9 seed, win a game in the tournament, and head home a minor hero. That's a good season. Coaching basketball at one of America's major universities and consistently putting one of the top sixty-eight college basketball teams on the court is a great way to keep your job. However, coaching football at one of those universities demands more. You have to be better than top 68, because being No. 40 might put your team in Boise, Idaho, for a bowl game rather than Pasadena or Miami. And that simply doesn't work. You do it too many times and you're gone.

Off the top of my head, I can name a dozen untouchable college basketball coaches: Coach K, Jim Boeheim, Roy Williams, Rick Pitino, Mark Few, Billy Donovan, Tom Izzo, Rick Barnes,

John Calipari, John Thompson III, Bill Self. They're the kings of the court. They're bigger than life. In some of them, the atmosphere creates incivility, arrogance, and a false feeling of omnipotence. They almost can't help it. Even college basketball coaches shrouded in controversy—Knight, Tarkanian, Calhoun—fight back like cornered raccoons. *They go after the school president.* Think about that. It's unbelievable.

I'm generalizing here, but that doesn't make it any less true. A college football coach who is in trouble—say, Mack Brown—is praying to survive. Even a legend like Bobby Bowden, who was just trying to get a few more wins and another year for his resume, would consider it outrageous to attack the school president.

It's hard to attach the word *humble* to Lane Kiffin, but why does Lane Kiffin text me repeatedly? Because Lane knows ultimately he has to win. He knows every game matters. In college football, each game is celebrated. It's a three-month sport, whereas college basketball has devolved into essentially a three-week sport. Lane's USC team was the consensus No. 1 entering the 2012 season, and the Trojans ended up playing in the Sun Bowl in El Paso. Do you think the USC boosters look at that and say, "Well, Lane made it to a bowl game, so it's a good year"? Of course not. It was a terrible year, and Lane knows it.

Here's what I find in life: when you combine a feeling of invincibility with a large salary, you create apathy and a lack of humility. In the case of college basketball coaches, those factors are combined with an almost fawning media, driven by various networks, including ESPN, that supports the worst-behaved coaches unconditionally. Put it all together and you've got the ingredients to manufacture petty tyrants and people who believe they're bigger than life.

Because if I'm Mr. Big-Time Basketball Coach, here's what I'm seeing: I've got the fawning media, I make my own schedule, I make the tournament, you pay me a fortune, and you can't fire me. I've got only one question: Where's my throne?

I don't feel that in the NBA, the NHL, Major League Baseball, or major college football. Even a baseball team like the low-payroll A's—take a look at them. Billy Beane treats baseball managers like yesterday's trash. Joe Girardi has to win or he's in danger of losing his job. Other than Buck Showalter, who is not on the hot seat? Bruce Bochy because he's won two of the last three World Series? Maybe, but he better not have two bad years in a row. Baseball managers are perpetually on the verge of being fired.

College basketball coaches are the most difficult and the most brittle. They're the most unwilling to compromise. They're the most defensive and combative when called on their behavior. And why not? An entire industry has been built up around their ability to control the young, mostly African-American athletes they recruit. And it's not just an industry—it's an aura. *This guy's a genius. That guy's a genius.* They have all this power and very little accountability. It's no wonder they start believing all the gushing praise that flows their way.

It's part of the culture, and the culture creates the personality.

My advice to young guys dreaming of the NBA? Focus on the J . . . um, not that J.

Drunk and Stupid: No Way to Go Through a Football Game

There's a bit I have on my radio show where I give my listeners a simple piece of advice if they find themselves pondering the sanity of a particular idea.

Say it out loud.

Get it out. Let it breathe. Judge its merits based on how it sounds when it hits the open air.

Certain concepts seem outrageous when exposed to the elements. Here's one: up until 1998, airline passengers in the United States were allowed to smoke on certain airline flights. It took until 2000 for the federal government to pass a law banning smoking on all United States passenger planes, regardless of length or destination.

This seems incomprehensible. Until April of 1998, we put people in a pressurized tube with recycled air and let smokers light up whenever they wanted. And that—somehow—was OK.

An airplane is a bundle of vital electrical systems. There are newspapers lying all over the place and fabric upholstery on the seats. But up until '98, you were allowed to hold a smoldering piece of carcinogenic *fire* between your fingers at 33,000 feet if the domestic flight was longer than six hours. All the FAA and TSA regulations we have to deal with now—you can't even bring a bottle of water onto a plane, or a 3.5-ounce stick of gel deodorant—and fifteen years ago you could pull out a lighter in 26E and blow cigarette smoke in the faces of the people on either side of you.

Say it out loud, and it sounds insane. Today, the thought of someone smoking in a warehouse or an enormous big-box store is unfathomable. The idea of smoking in an airplane? It's the most absurd notion in the world.

But we don't have to look very deeply into the sports world to find analogies. In this case, the ingredients are football, young men, and alcohol, and the mixture creates a concoction that is senseless, dangerous, and frightening.

Start with this: a growing number of universities are now selling alcohol in their on-campus football stadiums.

Say it out loud.

We're putting charged-up young males in supercharged environments and serving them alcohol. Of the 120 Division I football programs, 21 of them sell alcohol at their games, and 11 of those stadiums are on campus.

It doesn't sound like much, but think about the ramifications. As we know, binge drinking is a huge concern on college campuses, and nearly a dozen of those campuses are plying their students—the ones of legal drinking age, we assume—with alcohol during games.

College students start drinking on Thursday night. Are you telling me they can't take a three-and-a-half-hour hiatus on Saturday afternoon?

Say it out loud.

West Virginia started selling beer in its stadium in 2011, and the Associated Press reported the athletic department raised $520,000 in beer money. Is it worth it? You're willing to take on the insurance risk and potential public-relations hit for half a million dollars? Are you aware of how much money BCS schools are making off television revenue and bowl revenue? A half-million dollars is not do-or-die money for a BCS-level athletic program.

You have to ask yourself, what's the purpose? Notre Dame doesn't sell beer in the stands. Does that hurt the aura of Notre

Dame football? I've been to games across the country. I've been to Camp Randall at Wisconsin and the Horseshoe at Ohio State, two schools that play in a conference (the Big Ten) in which no schools, except Minnesota, sell alcohol in the regular seating areas. And you know what? Those places aren't suffering from a lack of enthusiasm or raucous behavior due to their not selling beer in the stands. It's still a party atmosphere, just as it is in every major college football stadium.

We're going to look back at this someday and say, "Wow—we were *completely* idiotic."

There's also a contradiction at work: the NCAA has no rules prohibiting sales at regular season events, but it bans the sale of alcohol and alcohol-related advertising during its eighty-eight championships. Additionally, host sites must cover up alcohol advertising during events. What does that tell you? Clearly, there are apprehensions within the NCAA about the connection between alcohol and college sports. It is saying, "We're uncomfortable about this at a high-profile event, but we can't do a whole lot if you want to sell it on campus."

We hear the same arguments every time the topic is raised. People are already drinking before and after games, so what's the difference? The undercurrent to that argument is this: Why shouldn't colleges reap some of the profits from what everyone knows is already happening?

A lot of people smoke in America, too. Does that mean we should encourage it, or not make an attempt to lessen it?

Another argument: college football and drinking have become synonymous, and it's foolish to try to stop it.

Well, fast food and obesity have become synonymous, too. Should we stop trying to educate people on that linkage? Should we go completely libertarian?

We know from a study conducted by the Institute of Alcohol Studies that 25 percent of binge drinkers commit violent offenses. On a more colloquial level, we know that alcohol plus young men equals trouble. Football games attract young men. Football games attract young men who like to drink. And *college* football games attract young men who are away from home for the first time and maybe drinking for the first time and doing stupid things out of their parents' line of sight for the first time. Geez, what could go wrong?

In the UK, they had a government-funded initiative to confiscate alcohol from kids 18 and under. The result? A 15 percent drop in crime. We all know the game here, and we all know the consequences. There's a gigantic risk involved in getting young men drunk enough to be idiots. Take a minute to go to YouTube and see the violence that takes place at football games. It's not pretty.

There's no part of this that makes sense. Universities should not be in the business of helping young men get drunk enough to be idiots. It's simply not worth the risk.

And I don't want to hear someone say, "You can't let a few people ruin it for everyone." Really? Yes, you can. That's the way laws work. We have laws throughout our country to restrict young men from doing something stupid. It's a logical means of protecting society from young men and young men from themselves. Look at car insurance—far more expensive for young men. Look at car-rental rules—can't rent a car until you're 25. Laws and rules are by definition restrictive. You can't be president till you're 35. You can't drive a car until you're 16. We have a concern about young men in America; they're the liability most insurance companies are concerned with. A nation of actuaries can't be wrong, can it?

But let's not limit this discussion to college football. The NFL has an alcohol problem, too, and its alcohol problem has the potential to become an economic problem. Right now, the NFL doesn't have too many money issues. In fact, it's almost impossible to find some part of the NFL that isn't increasing: television revenue, television ratings, endorsement deals, player salaries, training-camp crowds. And yet the one outlier is game attendance. Game attendance is declining. Blackouts are more common. The Raiders decided to tarp off the Mount Davis section of the Coliseum to reduce seating by 11,000 and make it easier to sell out.

Why? Why are more and more NFL fans staying home? You can run down the usual list of suspects: traffic hassles, ticket prices in a tough economy, high-definition television, the Red Zone channel.

But you have to leave room for one major reason: the behavior inside stadiums is appalling. From the language to the behavior to the sight of grown men peeing in bathroom sinks or garbage cans, NFL stadiums are quickly becoming places that are not in the least bit family-friendly.

Something has to be done about this. You go into an NFL stadium and the vulgarity is awful. A huge percentage of the crowd is hammered by the time it stumbles into the stadium, and now we're letting these guys leave parking lots just *smoked*. It's no surprise, though, because the NFL targets this crowd. And the NFL is making it worse by pushing more games late Sunday night, late Thursday night, the usual late Monday night. They're packing seventy thousand smashed people into a stadium and then sending them out on the interstate.

Say it out loud.

In many places, the macho, drunken, jersey-wearing fan feels he's upholding some unwritten code of local fandom if he gets as drunk as possible and defends his team's honor by getting into a fight. His language is vulgar, his mood is foul, and you better not stare at him for a millisecond too long or else he'll walk up on you and try to goad you into a fight.

This sounds horribly elitist—I admit it up front—but you can separate men into two categories: Job Guy or Career Guy. The NFL markets itself to blue-collar, working-class men. All the commercials—Budweiser, Ford trucks, Doritos. It's a man's world, and these men aren't eating organic spinach and driving Priuses (Pri-i?).

Generally speaking, Career Guy is not going to go to a game on a Sunday afternoon and put his career in jeopardy by doing something idiotic. This is anecdotal, and based on my experience dealing with sponsors and salespeople, and other professionals, but Career Guy is far less likely to risk his professional well-being in favor of a dozen shots of cheap tequila and an upper-deck brawl with a guy wearing a different-colored jersey. He's got clients, maybe, or an important meeting on Monday. It's a much bigger deal for Career Guy to show up for work on Monday morning with a raging hangover and a black eye than it is for Job Guy. You're generally not going to put your career in jeopardy by throwing a haymaker at a guy at a football game. It's simply not worth it.

Sad to say, there's not as much of a social stigma for Job Guy if he acts like a complete asshat in a public setting. If you've got a job at a warehouse and the guy behind you pops off, what do you give a shit? You've had nineteen jobs, and your honor or your team is more important than that job. Job Guy might throw the haymaker, consequences be damned.

Say it out loud.

It's reached the point where the behavior inside stadiums is so appalling I believe alcohol should be banned, with few exceptions. One exception I would make—and this is going to sound elitist one more time—is for suites. The suites are predominately for advertisers, and many of the advertisers are alcohol companies. Obviously, the more they advertise, the more the franchise—and its fans—benefits. It's a fine line; alcohol is big business in the NFL, but it's also the biggest contributor to negative fan behavior. The stakes are high. The league—or individual teams—would not only have to take a stand, it would have to take a stand that would cost it some money.

But look at the big picture: this is the one league that has every major broadcast network under contract. This is the one league that is financially solvent, from top to bottom, inside and out. This isn't the NBA, where a certain percentage of the teams lose money. This isn't big-league baseball, where Tampa and Oakland just can't draw. I wouldn't fault the NHL if it said banning alcohol was a hit it couldn't afford to take; $4 million for an owner in that league could mean the difference between red and black.

The NFL is in a category all its own. What are they making on beer sales? Seven million per team maybe? Hell, the Seahawks paid Matt Flynn $10 million to *not* play.

Make one thing clear: I'm not a moralist or some throwback Puritan who believes strong drink is the devil's brew. I'm in favor of legalizing pot and I own a wine store.

Morals aren't the issue.

Sanity is the issue. Common sense is the issue.

You will never see me wear a jersey to a game. Ever. Maybe my ego is just too big, but I would never wear another man's name on my back. That's my back, and I'm proud of it. I don't want my kids to see me idolizing someone else. Do you want them to idolize other people? You can be respectful of someone's work without slobbering over him or her.

There's just too much man worship in sports. Maybe it's our Western religion where we look up for answers while Eastern religion asks you to look within yourself, not idolize or worship someone else.

It's what brought down Penn State football. People allowed a man in his eighties to run a $400 million football program. That's not being an ageist—it's being a realist. Joe Paterno was not only injured twice during his last few years, he was so generationally out of touch, he didn't recognize how dangerous and inappropriate the Jerry Sandusky information was.

Never forget, Phil Jackson was once swept out of the playoffs. The late Steve Jobs at Apple had several creations that failed. Go look up his 1988 single-button mouse, which could have doubled as a hockey puck.

When Bill Belichick and the Patriots acquired Tim Tebow, there was immediate recognition of Belichick's brilliance. How soon we forget his dubious acquistions of Albert Haynesworth and Chad Ochocinco and his regrettable trade of talented Richard Seymour.

Women seem to grow out of it. Teenage girls may worship boy bands or movie stars but move past the infatuation at an earlier age. With guys, it starts early and often grows when we have the means to support it. Autographs, iPhone pictures, fantasy camps, message boards, paying thousands for a seat at a table with a 67-year-old former football star—would a woman really pay 25 grand for a dinner with Molly Ringwald in 2013?

Man worship is at an all-time high. It's a bull market right now. No thanks.

Holding a grudge is the equivalent of chain-smoking hate.

Hanging in the Imbalance

Bel Air Country Club is nestled into the hills above UCLA's campus in one of the most prestigious neighborhoods in the country, and it's just as beautiful as it sounds.

After a round of golf at Bel Air, it's not uncommon to spot anyone—from a broadcasting icon to a business tycoon to a Hollywood celebrity—knocking back a few. On the night of my one and only visit, I spotted all of the above when former NBA player and coach Mike Dunleavy invited me up for a few drinks before he and his wife went to dinner elsewhere.

The next ninety minutes were filled with giant laughs, compelling stories, and a sense of camaraderie among men who may find themselves competing against one another during the work week. These were men who put in long hours, and this impromptu 6:15 cocktail party was a break from lives filled with deadlines and pressure. No one, judging by the conversations, would be happy living his life any other way. They were competitive, hardworking guys, and nobody was about to apologize for that.

I had put in a long week of radio shows and sales meetings. Before I sat down with Mike and entered into the group conversation, I was dragging. Within minutes, I was energized.

It was the same energy I feel whenever I'm in a room full of athletes, coaches, or other dreaded type-A personalities who are often criticized for lacking balance, priorities, and a sense of perspective.

These are men and women—mostly men, to be honest—who are often singularly obsessed with achievement or mission. The problem, according to too many people who lack the same drive, is that people like this lack *balance*.

You've heard it:

He's a workaholic. His life is out of balance.
He's obsessed. He needs some balance in his life.

Is it possible that this premise—one of our longest-held and least-questioned—is mostly one giant crock?

If you live in my world long enough, it certainly feels that way.

I decided to research what makes people happy, and I found that even chronically unhappy people don't list *a balanced life* as a means of escaping from the dark tunnel of depression. Of all the things listed—independence, sex, achievement, charity work, exercise—*balance* was nowhere to be found.

How can that be? How can such a vital and universally acknowledged key to happiness not be, in fact, a key to happiness? My barista is a poet, web designer, ski bum, and all-around radical dude—he *always* has a lively step to his mornings.

Could it be possible that Peyton Manning, a guy who spends countless hours breaking down game film without so much as a single camping trip with his buddies or a visible recreational pursuit, may be just as happy as my barista? Or—gulp—even *more* so?

I can only speak for guys since . . . well, I am one. But after forty-nine years on this planet, most of it spent observing and then discussing teams and people, I'm going rogue right here: Unbalanced Guy? He's doing just fine.

You can have Balanced Guy. I'll take his miserable brother, otherwise known as "Fully Committed to Something." You'll recognize him if you see him. He's the one always hanging out with another unbalanced guy—"You Get One Shot at This Life and I'm Going to Make Something of It."

Maybe those guys get home every night and head to the nearest sofa, where they dive headfirst, bury themselves in designer throw pillows, and sob for hours.

Or maybe they don't.

Maybe through intense competition on the climb to the top of their fields, they've grown accustomed to—but not comfortable with—the occasional defeat and are resilient enough that the kind of day-to-day problems that derail most people are treated as welcome challenges.

Here's a question for every therapist who preaches balance: Would you prefer balance from the quarterback of your favorite NFL team? You know, the guy who might have had a better game if he hadn't spent several hours that week on his new whittling exhibit? If you're a therapist in Dallas and a Cowboys' season-ticket holder, would you prefer Tony Romo to skip practice today to work on his recently acquired interest in the violin?

Nobody is suggesting that staring at a computer screen all day is a recipe for eternal bliss. Nobody is suggesting you ignore your kids, never take a vacation, and treat your spouse like an employee. Nobody is saying that having the Unabomber's social life is the way to go.

But look around. You'll see a pattern.

As author Scott H. Young writes, "Almost everything meaningful is accomplished by a megalomaniac on a mission. Balance is static, it's the opposite of change and growth. Obsession, not balance, makes things happen."

Isn't it reasonable, then, to assume that many people or groups who create everything from transcendent technological advances to small landscaping companies gain a level of self-worth that wouldn't have been possible without some level of obsession?

Unless you're reading this book in Yellowstone National Park, look around right now. What do you see—a computer, a house, a nice clock, dual-pane windows? You think Balanced Guy made all those things happen? And if you acknowledge that Unbalanced Guy was the driving force behind them, don't you think he gained something emotionally from his creations?

In sports, teams are constantly asking for more from you, the fan. Rising ticket prices, PSLs, $9 beers, DirecTV packages to watch games—they're on a mission to separate you from your discretionary income. Given that, isn't it perfectly fine for you to ask for something in return, like a greater and more serious commitment from the athletes and coaches your team employs?

For one thing, it pays off. Longtime NFL scout Gary Horton told me the hardest-working coach he ever met was Bill Belichick. Upon being hired to coach the Cleveland Browns, Belichick gathered every scout in a room and broke down what he wanted from a nose tackle should the Browns ever draft one.

This nose-tackle meeting took more than four hours.

Horton said Ravens general manager Ozzie Newsome, maybe the league's most respected talent evaluator, has a relentless work ethic. Newsome arrives at the office every morning in the off-season to watch tapes of college players, many of whom the Ravens have no chance of landing.

Maybe it's just a vicious cycle, and we're all to blame for the unbalance in our lives. We pay more, therefore we demand more and we're all miserable in the process. Is that how it works? Maybe an 8-8 team makes the world a happier and more balanced place, enough wins to bring me—the fan—back, but not so many wins that the coaching staff won't take that extra weekend off.

But what are the sports stories we want to hear? From my

lengthy experience in the field, I've got a pretty good idea: Michael Jordan lifting weights the morning after every game of his career; Kobe Bryant refusing to leave the practice gym until he wins the final game of H-O-R-S-E; Peyton Manning sitting in a dark film room hours after practice looking for the slimmest edge on his opponent.

For all we give to sports, these are the stories we *need* to hear.

Nearly any business of any size—sports teams and leagues included—resides in a global space. Fifty years ago, the great 18-year-old American shortstop had to worry about fewer competitors for a job in the big leagues. Now, that same kid has to be better than shortstops from the Dominican Republic, Venezuela, Mexico, and even Cuba.

You simply can't rise to the highest level without putting in more hours than your competitors. And when it comes to sports, the more hours you put in at an earlier age, all the better.

In 1996, the late writer David Foster Wallace wrote a fascinating article in *Esquire* about a little-known tennis player named Michael Joyce, who was the seventy-ninth-ranked player in the world at the time. Wallace delved into the inner workings of the tennis circuit and told the story through Joyce's eyes, and one thing became abundantly clear: the commitment, time, and focus needed to be a top 100 player—even in the second half of that top 100—is not suited for those who are only partially devoted to the sport. As Wallace writes, "The realities of top level athletics today require an early and total commitment to one area of excellence. An ascetic focus. A consent to live in a world that's very small."

The question then becomes, does that small world necessarily make you less happy?

A 2006 Pew survey attempted to define happiness as it pertains to political persuasion, always a dicey proposition. But the findings were illuminating. The survey found that conservatives, regardless of income level, are happier than liberals. (This indicates that the prevailing idea that older, wealthier conservatives are happier than younger liberals is true but not exclusively true.)

The study used political persuasion while basing its findings on the well-established Big Five personality scale, in which five factors—openness, conscientiousness, extraversion, agreeableness, and neuroticism—are used to determine personality.

What did it find? Conservatives tend to be less neurotic and fretful. They don't agonize over unknowns, which means they probably don't lose sleep over the possible tyranny of a third-world dictator. The study concluded that conservatives know their place in the universe and aren't troubled by it.

Liberals, on the other hand, need closure and certainty. They *are* troubled by the tyranny of a third-world dictator, even though they are undoubtedly powerless to do anything about it. They focus on what is idealized rather than what is possible, while conservatives focus on stability and community, two factors that are far more controllable.

I'm not suggesting the path to happiness starts with trading Rachel Maddow for Sean Hannity. I doubt psychologists and therapists are touting their new treatment—Beat depression! Watch *Fox News*!—as better than medication. The conservative/liberal thing is a mind-set that extends beyond politics, and the study left me with an overwhelming sense that a smaller world with more certainty makes people happier. Maybe that seems counterintuitive in an increasingly global community, but one finding of the study struck a chord with me: conservatives cared more about community than liberals, but it was limited to the community that they consider theirs.

And that phenomenon—the world-within-a-world—is what I have witnessed for more than twenty years in sports. Hyperfocused people living goal-oriented lives attain levels of confidence as a direct result of their familiarity with success.

Despite their seemingly single-minded devotion, they love their families and have friends. But on a deeper level, they're searching for personal achievement, a way of putting a stamp on their lives. They have no guilt about it, no qualms about setting goals and going balls-out to achieve them.

They aren't choosing the local triathlon over feeding their kids. At the same time, they know they can't feed all the world's starving children, so they aren't going to worry about it. Would they be better served if they *did* become overwhelmed by the plight of all the starving children in the world, to the point of making themselves depressed and miserable over it?

Conservatives cry, too, but for them all crying is local.

Like any industry, the top of the sports food chain is filled with serious people who have pruned away life's excess branches at an early age. They've found jobs and projects they love, and they've set out to create a path they can control to achieve goals that are within reach. They seek the kind of certainty a relentless work ethic can make possible.

And if that means they sacrifice balance along the way, they don't care. They've found something more important: results.

Balance, dare I say it, is vastly overrated.

In the end, you might want to consider the benefits of imbalance, and the achievements that come with pursuing a passion with single-minded devotion.

You can continue to seek balance. By all means, go right ahead and marvel at the balance of your life as you stand over the bean dip at your fourth dinner party this week.

If you can stare into that dip and see the path to the kind of happiness that comes with long days and constant pressure and daily competition, more power to you.

When people say that if college athletes aren't paid they are being extorted, all I can say is, would someone please extort my kids to Stanford?

For Adults Only

It's not one of the world's more pressing concerns, but if you travel regularly, you know that every major airline has turned the boarding process into one of the more ridiculous events in human history. The whole operation has jumped not only the shark but also the manatees and squid. It's rapidly making its way through every other living sea creature.

There was a time, lo those many years ago, when people who purchased first-class tickets or had frequent-flier upgrades to first class boarded . . . well, you know . . . *first*. Oh, the gimpy octogenarian fresh off hip surgery also got the early invite, but now the rules are completely different. All bets are off.

Now? Now it's pretty much a free-for-all. Gone are the days of purchasing or earning an early walk down the jetway. Now boarding early is looked upon as the God-given right of anyone who's had so much as a leg cramp or an ice-cream headache in the past week.

"Anyone with a first-class ticket, people with children, mimes, those who feel a little gassy, women named after months, and people who watched the final episode of Arrested Development— *all of you are welcome to board early."*

Since children won't read this book and are the easiest to pick on, can we just start—and end—with them?

Can someone please tell me why six-year-old Amber needs to board first? Does she have a big meeting at Lego to attend? Is there a Disney Princess Convention I'm not aware of?

Look, I'm a proud parent. I'm not antikid by any means. However, that doesn't mean that responsible and sane adults should encourage children to fly.

Yes, I just said that.

Parents considering taking their young kids on cross-country flights should feel the same way left-handed batters did when facing Randy Johnson in his prime: it's probably safe, but don't push your luck.

In other words, when you're at the plate, lean back, not forward.

It would be dangerous and irresponsible for us to make the childhood flying experience so darned plum-tastic that kids inform other kids. We'd be risking some sort of child revolution that we'd have to battle the rest of our lives.

I'll tell you what we need to do: we need to make the flying experience fall somewhere between being sent to your room and having to eat all the hideous frozen mixed vegetables Mom just dumped on your plate. You know, the ones she dished out while wearing a slightly devilish smile.

Because let's face it: once word gets out that spending a few hours in one of those winged metal things is no day at the theme park, we'll pretty much eliminate the kind of whining that could possibly lead to a six-day trip toward sunshine.

Settle down, mom-zealots. Nobody here is suggesting kids should board last and sit right next to those loud jet engines. Although I've got to think rows 28–34 are about the best place to put them. After all, planes don't back into mountains, right?

And nobody is suggesting that kids can't spend the entire flight stuffing their faces with however many pounds of junk you packed in that duffel bag. Although it's worth noting that kids have small stomachs, and a glass of warm milk on an empty stomach might help kick-start a nap.

I'm just pleading for reason here. As the self-appointed president of Citizens for a Slightly More Rigid Boarding Process, I'm just throwing out some ideas for discussion.

There's no reason to get all upset. We're all on the same page.

Or should be.

Everyone wins with quieter planes—especially busy radio hosts who, if disrupted, could lose valuable prep time and come into work groggy and cranky.

Or who knows what else.

I also understand something important about why kids fly: grandparents miss their grandchildren. They need those annual visits and look forward to them. And that's why, as a public service, I'd like to propose another civic organization to join my brilliant Citizens for a Slightly More Rigid Boarding Process.

The new group? Cheaper Seats for Grandparents Who Want to See Their Grandkids But Can't Because They're on a Limited Budget.

See where I'm going here?

Two birds, one stone.

I admit, my initial tone was fairly harsh. By now, though, I'm confident you can see my heart is in the right place.

And that right place is Row One, Seat A, surrounded only by adults.

Fit is underrated.

When I used to work in local news you would see one popular anchor get plucked away by the rival news team. He or she would get a fat new contract and it was all the talk of the town among the media. Yet they never delivered the same ratings magic. Why? It's so obvious, but news managers continue making the same hiring mistakes. It's about the fit, not the face.

News teams that win the ratings war all deliver a certain comfort or chemistry to the viewer. The members of these teams appear, at least, to like one another. The new well-compensated, polished news anchor is now on an imaginary pedestal. He doesn't feel like one of the guys. He's a hired gun.

An intruder, almost.

In life, finding that perfect fit is difficult and underrated. They say everybody has an interesting story to tell and I would add this: they also have a gift if they can discover it and polish it. They just need the right fit. Even people who appear to be unmotivated have a fit.

Take Pot Dealer Guy.

About once or twice a year you see one of these stories hit the front pages:

A 36-year-old high school dropout who lives over his mom's garage is running a sophisticated marijuana ring.

As you read the story your jaw drops. The same dude who refused to wear a belt or tie to his brother's wedding is now the driving force behind a $234 million hydroponic pot farm with an intricate irrigation system that is the envy of most agricultural centers.

What in the name of Cheech, Chong, and Jeff Spicoli is going on?

What's going on? Pot guy found his fit. It wasn't in corporate America and isn't even legal in America. But he found it.

Fit happens. Make it happen for you. Legally, of course.

Bowling is the only sport where the better you are, the less attractive you become to the opposite sex.

Leaving Las Vegas

What happens when your trip down memory lane takes a detour that doesn't make its way down a lane after all? What if, instead of a lane, it's a strip—a strip full of sex pamphlets, drunks, and Elvis impersonators?

There are all sorts of things you can lose in Las Vegas, but for me the city isn't defined by what I left behind but by what stayed with me. No matter how many showers you take, something is bound to stick to you once you leave.

The city provides opportunities to unearth the buried truth in all of us. In Vegas, you can take your reckless judgment out for a walk. You can invite yourself into any and all kinds of oddball encounters. You can be as dangerous and uninhibited as you want.

Vegas simply lobs the pitch over the heart of the plate and begs you to swing away. For me, the place is truth serum covered in neon.

I was fortunate enough to land my first broadcasting job in Las Vegas in 1986, back before it became the monorailed, corporatized, culinary hot spot it is today.

It was headlined by the three Ts: Tyson, Tark, and Trouble. The Mob still had an active presence and the growth spurt was just beginning. The city's, that is—not mine.

Tark, of course, is shorthand for Jerry Tarkanian, the former UNLV basketball coach who both fascinated and bothered me in equal measure. Most broadcasters begin their careers covering minor-league teams. Mine began covering the nation's most controversial coach.

Anywhere.

Ever.

He and I had our differences, but I've never met anyone in sports like Tark the Shark. He was a really good man. Or maybe he wasn't. I can go either way.

To say Tarkanian was complex would be like calling Fenway Park an old sandlot. Tark would be brought to tears by children and was known to interrupt a recruiting session by telling a young prospective UNLV Rebel that he would be better off going to Stanford rather than his public desert institution. He once told a luncheon crowd he loved taking his teams to tournaments in Hawaii because most black players don't want to hang out at the beach. He said it without an ounce of malice but instead with the authority of someone who—after twenty-five years of coaching—was simply relaying something he perceived to be an absolute.

One of his favorite pastimes was criticizing coaches who lamented the recruiting process. As he saw it, "You get paid to watch basketball in the day and eat steaks and drink beer at night on the university's dime. What's so hard about that?"

He was the most honest coach I ever covered.

Sometimes.

Tark had a personal valet/shadow named Mike Toney who was straight out of central casting. Toney wore cheap sweat suits with the same deluded pride Ronny from *Jersey Shore* wore his fake tan. One of Toney's jobs was to handle Tarkanian's enormous, contractually negotiated ticket allotment from the school. During his peak years, when the Runnin' Rebels were routinely in the national-title conversation, that allotment was pure gold and he was sitting on a mountain of it. Whatever Tark wanted he bartered for, or at least Toney did. Anyone who covered the program during that period knew it was an ugly scheme, but we weren't IRS agents. And frankly, some of Tark's allies had all the charm of Paulie Walnuts.

The Rebels' starting five, despite coming from some less-than-ideal backgrounds, drove nicer cars than the media members who covered them. Yet for the bench players—the guys who were six through twelve on the roster—it was the same beat-up Datsuns or creaky bicycles popular with the rest of the student body.

Convicted points shaver Richie "The Fixer" Perry in a hot tub with UNLV players might have seemed outrageous to the national press, but I had only one question: Was it the players' hot tub, or Richie's?

This wasn't Iowa State. Then again, Vegas isn't Ames.

Tarkanian argued with me one day about the players he recruited. Some of them had checkered backgrounds, but Tark's voice rose as he told me his kids just deserved a chance in life and that they'd never hurt a soul.

His voice grew reflective when he asked, "Without opportunities, where would I be?"

He was a really good guy that day.

Or maybe he wasn't.

John Henderson covered the program at the time for the *Las Vegas Review-Journal*. He once came home after writing a negative story to find his apartment trashed. He never found out who did it, but we all had our suspicions that it was connected to his not-always-glowing coverage of Tark and the Runnin' Rebels. I got anonymous death threats on my voicemail and was angrily confronted in grocery stores for commentaries that were considered anti-Tark.

Tark's response to all of this? "Some of the fans are a little crazy," he said, smiling and shaking his head.

He preferred media coverage that was close enough to hear his thoughts but distant enough to . . . well . . . just distant enough. Leave it at that.

Without knowing it, Tarkanian provided a helpful glimpse at

how complex people can be. Like Tark, none of us are one thing; we're a collection of conflicts. We're all good in our own ways and troublesome in others. Tarkanian was different only in the way he wore his conflicts right out in the open, on his trademark short-sleeved shirts.

He was both caring and callous, loyal and self-serving, modest and egomaniacal.

Even the NCAA seemed conflicted on how to handle Tarkanian. After he sued the institution for harassment after repeated investigations, the NCAA settled on a $2.5 million payout but refused to admit it was actually guilty of harassment.

I know how the NCAA felt. Covering the man for six years was similar to riding a roller coaster: you're exhilarated while it's happening, glad and relieved when it's over.

All of these years later, what am I to think of Tark? Or should I look at it another way and just thank him for making me think?

Bobby Knight condemns coaches who manipulate the system. Knight is regarded as a squeaky clean arbiter of collegiate ethics. But look at his methods—he bullied everyone from students to officials to athletic-department personnel.

So, is Knight the good guy or is Tark?

Both?

Neither?

Tark leaves me as conflicted today as I was while covering him and his teams.

Two years ago at a Penn State radio remote, his nieces approached me and said Jerry insisted they stop by and say hello. He had nothing to gain. The gesture felt genuine.

Despite everything, I think Tark was really a good man.

There are others who think, *You know what? Maybe he wasn't.*

Is it a copout for me to say I understand both sides? Because I do. I understand how Tark could be a cold, all-consuming coach who constantly fought The Man and tried to bend the rules in his direction. I also understand how Tark tried to bend those rules and fight that fight because he truly cared about the poor and disadvantaged kids who came to play in his program.

It makes sense that Tark's nieces—years after our contentious relationship ended—would be asked to relay a kind message from their uncle. By that time, he was no longer coaching and I was no longer a threat. Once upon a time, we both had a job to do, and each of us understood the other within that context.

It's a perspective I don't ever want to lose, and I have Tark to thank for the lesson.

People say they want something but sometimes are better served without it. Transparency comes to mind.

Politicians say they'll deliver it. Your boss promises he'll manage with it. Maybe sometimes we're just better off not knowing things.

Everybody knows that CEO pay is out of control in many sectors. The big guy is making way too much compared to the average worker. At least too much for most people's taste. The vitriol, though, has ramped up in recent years.

People don't seem to get nearly as agitated over this fact: 60 percent of corporations are not paying taxes. Yet you can't put a singular face to that. At least that rich CEO is ponying up a large chunk to the IRS.

I would argue part of that current animosity over wealth isn't just about the gap between rich and poor, but it's also due to an expanded media, where we see and hear daily how we all stack up. From the Internet to social media, blogs, and reality shows on every other cable channel, we get lavish lifestyles poured into our glass nightly and hourly. You see the faces of wealth.

It's one thing to have a more successful family member, but what if he was your neighbor? What if you had to watch him routinely upgrading his landscaping—the kind you only wish you could afford? What if he pulled into the driveway with a new SUV every twelve months while your 1993 model was in and out of the shop? Sometimes the harsh truth isn't that much fun when it's pushed into your face.

Animosity and jealousy, two very ugly words, only arrive after disclosure. The same goes for sorrow and heartbreak.

If God didn't really exist, is the public better off knowing that? Don't many people rely on that existence for comfort and guidance?

There's a reason the media doesn't televise suicides. We don't need to see it. Nobody really does. Whose life is really elevated by seeing someone else take theirs?

We often demand total transparency but, number one, total transparency doesn't exist, and two, we're all probably happier if we don't know everything about everything.

Sports stars are the royalty in this country. England has the Queen, we have shooting guards.

IQ, Low-Q, No Clue

I hereby present two words no guy wants to read:

Menstrual synchrony.

It's an unproven theory most guys don't know about, and those who *do* know about it would rather not discuss it.

Don't bother looking it up. I already did.

The theory suggests that menstrual cycles of women who live together—in homes, convents, prisons—can become synchronized over time. The concept first came to the public's attention in 1971, in an article in *Nature* magazine that studied the menstrual cycles of young women in a college dormitory. Supposedly women can sense the pheromones of other women and eventually their cycles synchronize, like an airborne virus.

Menstrual synchrony was brought to my attention years ago by a female friend who happened to play college basketball. She swore it was true. Research is split on whether it's a scientifically verifiable phenomenon, and frankly I would like to move on, regardless of the evidence.

But it does get me to my point: If it's possible for women to share such an experience, isn't it also true for men?

I would say it is, but unfortunately for men, the "shared experience" is far more embarrassing.

Because for men, the experience is stupidity.

Anytime you get more than three men together in a room, on a golf trip, on a Las Vegas weekend, at a poker game, in a bar, or at a ballgame, it's a virtual certainty that one of them will morph into a cross between Johnny Knoxville and Andy Dick.

It's a $2.99 testosterone combo deal, with a side of moron.

Even smart, thoughtful men can't help but lose fifty IQ points in the company of other men.

Would any guy—by himself—jump off the roof of a house?

Nope.

Would any guy—by himself—light a bottle rocket in his hand?

Nope.

But that just described Daniel Tosh's television career.

I know: let's find four or five guys, turn on a camera, and give them beer. The rest, I guarantee you, will be a waterslide through Neanderthal hell.

When NBA center Jason Collins became the first active player in a major American sport to come out as gay, the news was illuminating in so many ways. The announcement shed light on small-minded bigots and open-minded NBA stars such as Kobe Bryant and Steve Nash.

More than anything, though, it showed just how little we think of groups of men. I mean, *Wow.* It's just amazing how little regard we have for men who congregate in groups.

For one, they're dangerous. For another, they're stupid.

And that's just the beginning.

It might be hard to believe, but immediately after Collins's announcement, the story shifted to focus on how men might react to another man's sexual orientation. This idea—that a man within one of these hypermacho groups might be attracted to other men—was so unsettling that it consumed the narrative.

How will this be viewed within the NBA community?
How do players feel about the possibility of playing with
    a gay man?
Will teammates feel funny showering with him?

Will teammates, fearing that people may question their
sexuality, shun him?

By the way, it's worth noting that players on six different teams over the course of twelve NBA seasons had already been showering next to this guy long before he made his historic announcement. So there's that.

It's also instructive to note that this problem—or perceived problem—was limited to groups of men. In other words, the guys who gather together and end up jumping out of a window or blowing up a firework in their hands.

Individually, men have handled this alleged issue just fine.

Greg Louganis, the Olympic diver, announced he was gay and nobody seemed to care much. Of course, he was in an individual sport, where men weren't coming together in a big group to act like idiots. When it's a team sport, where a collection of men engages in low-level *groupthink,* somebody better call security. We could have a problem here.

We all know that men, especially young men, commit most of the crime in any country. The likelihood of arrest for men rises sharply in the late teens and remains high through the early twenties before dropping off when marriage and families and a decrease in testosterone brings some sanity to the proceedings.

But consider the poor opinion that society has of young men. They can go to war, vote for the leader of the free world, but can't rent a car before 25 or drink a beer legally until 21. Essentially, society feels it has to babysit you young fellas. We've installed layers of rules and laws to stop you from hurting yourself—and us.

Your parents must be proud.

That's not to say that groups of men can't be heroic or capable of great things. But it seems like those great things are always framed within an organization that prides itself on the leadership and guidance of older men. Think about military groups or sports teams; they're supervised and motivated by older, wiser men who are less prone to the irrational antics of the childish and impulsive.

Left to their own devices, young men all too often fall into the sad and pathetic frat mentality.

Not even our smart and civilized neighbors to the north are immune from this dynamic. The conclusion of the 2011 Stanley Cup Finals between the Vancouver Canucks and Boston Bruins got ugly. The Bruins beat the Canucks and a riot erupted in the streets of Vancouver. An eyewitness reported hearing a group of young men (of course) chanting, "Let's go riot!" In the end, more than 140 people were hurt, more than 100 were arrested, and the property damage estimate hit $4.2 million.

What's hockey's main demographic?

Young men.

Obviously.

You can picture the scene, can't you?

Hey man, we just lost. I think the only thing that could make me feel better is to light a Chevy on fire.

That's the mentality that creates concern for Jason Collins's future as an active athlete. In his profession, he can't help but be surrounded by groups of young men who are so consumed with protecting and promoting their masculinity that they become incapable of common decency and tolerance.

Guys, it's time to grow—and grow up.

People want me to give their team credit. I'm not in the credit business; Visa is. I'm in the honesty business and I may not like your team.

Michael vs. LeBron:
Swish or Swoosh?

Michael Jordan is the most popular and revered athlete in the world. He is absolutely glorified as a global icon, to the point where his fiftieth birthday in February of 2013 caused the sports media to reach for new ways to cover what is essentially a nonevent.

LeBron James, on the other hand, is one of the most polarizing athletes in the world. Any of his missteps, or perceived missteps, is exaggerated. His flaws, or perceived flaws, are dwelled on long after they've been either rectified or proven wrong. *The Decision* is a running joke that may end up being the second or third line of his obituary.

Why? Why are two of the four or five greatest basketball players in the history of the game treated so differently? Is Jordan so morally superior that he deserves no criticism while the other is so morally reprehensible he deserves it all?

No. Far from it. Couldn't be further from the truth.

To accurately assess the phenomenon, start with one word: Nike.

I am in no way insinuating that Michael Jordan didn't do his part to fuel his popularity. But part of his appeal—a *big* part of his appeal—is that he had the greatest marketing ever put forth on behalf of an athlete.

Marketing creates popularity, and popularity creates a shield. Nobody on earth—nobody in the *history* of the earth—is marketed more thoroughly and effectively than Michael Jordan. It's not even close. Nike is the only company that can create a marketing campaign that drives public opinion. And that's not open for debate, either.

The type of campaign Nike runs creates an army of people who do the groundwork. They spread the word. They defend against all critics. This army of evangelists works in concert with the larger campaign to create an airtight, indestructible image.

It's nothing less than a real-life superpower.

If you have it, nothing can penetrate. If you don't, you're going to have a hard time shedding anything even remotely negative.

Take USC football coach Lane Kiffin. He's unpopular for any number of reasons. He got too much too soon when Al Davis hired him to be the youngest head coach in the NFL. He was an ingrate when he dared to question Grandpa Al's football acumen after being fired by the Raiders. He's considered cocky and egomaniacal. He remains Public Enemy No. 1 in Tennessee for the slippery way he left his job as head coach of the Volunteers. Kiffin is not always deft when it comes to public relations, so everything sticks to him. Big stuff, little stuff—doesn't matter. If it went wrong, blame Lane. The Trojans were part of a ball-deflating scandal in 2012. He knew nothing about it and had nothing to do with it. He got blamed.

Unpopular guy: everything sticks.

Popular guy: nothing sticks.

We hold these truths to be self-evident.

The closest comparison to Jordan is Ronald Reagan. His "marketing" campaign was a political movement that anointed him to save the country after Jimmy Carter, and the movement served as his Nike. Reagan was an immensely popular president, and his popularity was remarkably persistent. It withstood despite Iran-Contra, losing 241 Marines in Lebanon, and goofy jokes about bombing the Soviet Union. What did Reagan's popularity get him? A lifetime—and beyond—pass that led the country to consider putting him on Mount Rushmore. Nothing could touch Saint Ronnie, and his popularity made him be known as The Teflon President.

Michael Jordan is the Ronald Reagan of the sports world.

He punched two teammates in practice sessions.

Didn't stick.

He called Kwame Brown a homosexual slur.

Didn't stick.

He was serially unfaithful to his wife.

Didn't stick.

He left the NBA during his prime in a frivolous attempt to pursue a baseball career amid rumors and allegations that he was forced out because of gambling problems.

Didn't stick.

He gave an outrageously petty Hall of Fame speech, going so far as to ridicule an old man who had the audacity to keep him on the junior varsity team when he was a sophomore in high school.

Didn't stick.

He is one of the most ineffective, even *inept,* decision-makers as president of the Charlotte Bobcats.

Didn't stick.

Indestructible and invincible must be a pretty cool way to go through life.

To make one thing clear: Jordan was the best basketball player I ever saw, but Nike created a mythical figure, where flaws disappear and attributes take on legendary status.

Jordan is the first athlete to literally become his own brand. It's almost laughable when you say it out loud: *the man is his own brand.* How powerful is that? Consider this: the most recognizable player in Major League Baseball, the best player in the biggest market with the best image—*Derek Jeter*—wears baseball spikes with a silhouette of Michael Jordan on them. The most well-known baseball player wears a basketball player's shoe. *That's* some serious power.

LeBron, despite talent that is in the same neighborhood as Jordan's, doesn't have anything close to the marketing power behind him. Because of that, he doesn't have anything close to the same impenetrable force field surrounding him.

Nike doesn't need to turn LeBron into another Jordan. They still have Jordan to be Jordan.

When Nike started its marketing push with Jordan, it needed him. Nike was already a multinational company, but the late '80s and early '90s were a different time. The landscape wasn't as cluttered. There weren't hundreds of television channels; there was no YouTube, no Internet. A company like Nike could still drive pop culture with clever advertising campaigns like the ones they ran for Jordan.

How strong is Nike? Nike is a company so profoundly shrewd that it could take a geographically isolated college football program from a state that produces, on average, five Division I players a year, and turn it into one of the top ten brands in college football. You want to know Nike's true power? Look no further than University of Oregon football.

Oregon football is a national brand. When I mention that program, you immediately think of a million different uniform combinations, an offense that runs a zillion miles per hour, and facilities that would make a Saudi prince blush.

All because Nike created the brand.

Here's another example: Reebok spent $50 million to be the title sponsor of the 1996 Summer Olympics in Atlanta. But when asked afterward to name the title sponsors, 22 percent of respondents to a survey said Nike, and 16 percent said Reebok.

How did Nike pull this off? In its usual smart, shrewd manner. It handed out swoosh placards in the venues and put giant billboards all over town. It put enormous swooshes on office buildings and skyscrapers in downtown Atlanta, so whenever there was a television shot of the city, there was sure to be a Nike swoosh in it.

Let's look a little closer at Michael and LeBron.

From the moment Michael hit the last-second shot for North Carolina to win the NCAA title his freshman year to the time he won his first NBA championship, eight years passed.

Eight years. Remember that.

From the time he graduated from high school, LeBron spent eight years trying to get an NBA title—six of them with a Cleveland team that had nobody else who even resembled a star—and it was seen as a huge character flaw. He wasn't a winner, he didn't care, he choked when it counted. LeBron was viewed as being more frivolous than Michael, less focused, the product of a generation that valued flash and cash over banners in the rafters.

Eight years for Michael, he became known as the ultimate winner.

Eight years for LeBron, and his inability to win was seen as a huge character flaw and proof that he really didn't care about winning.

Michael was focused. LeBron was frivolous.

The Michael vs. LeBron argument is almost entirely driven by what Nike created.

Even now, even after LeBron has won back-to-back titles and has reached the Finals in all three years with the Heat, his achievements get minimized because he is seen as orchestrating a championship by leaving—no, *betraying*—Cleveland for the title-ready roster in Miami.

That's the criticism: he had to leave to get his championships.

Excuse me, but isn't mobility *celebrated* in this country?

Not everywhere, and definitely not in every instance.

Oh, we celebrate the guy who worked at Starbucks and left

to start Peet's Coffee, but when it comes to sports we turn that on its head and vilify a guy who leaves a stagnant Cleveland team—for *less* money—to join a team with a better chance of winning a championship.

Joe Girardi went from managing the Marlins to managing the Yankees. Does anybody criticize him? No, he simply left for a better opportunity. Everyone seems to understand that—in most cases. Not in LeBron's, however.

The power of marketing can be seen in other sports. Everyone loves Peyton Manning more than Tom Brady, even though Brady has three Super Bowl wins and two Super Bowl MVPs while Manning has one Super Bowl win. (Jordan, by the way, seems to judge everyone by titles won, as evidenced by his contention that he'd take Kobe Bryant over LeBron because he has more NBA championships.) Why is Manning more popular? One reason: he has more and funnier commercials, which means he has a better image.

Why does Derrick Rose sell tons of sneakers while Tim Duncan sells none? Because Adidas has created an effective and widespread marketing campaign around Rose—who has limited success in the NBA playoffs—and Duncan couldn't care less about any of that stuff. It doesn't matter that Duncan is one of the best players in NBA history and has won four NBA titles.

Again, Jordan made a lot of his own breaks. But he didn't win any titles until he was teamed with Phil Jackson and Scottie Pippen. And look at these numbers: the year he retired for the first time, the Bulls went from fifty-seven wins with him to fifty-five without him. Nobody's saying he wasn't the most important player on that team, the difference between an NBA title and a flame-out in the playoffs, but the fact remains: fifty-seven with him, fifty-five without him.

LeBron's final year in Cleveland, the Cavs won sixty-one games. The next year, they won nineteen. *Nineteen*. They dropped forty-two games and went from having the best record in the NBA to getting the No. 1 pick in the draft.

Let's look at two specific charges at LeBron:

1. He's a quitter. This stems from the 2010 Eastern Conference Semifinals, James's last games in Cleveland. Cavaliers owner Dan Gilbert was quoted as saying, "He quit in games two, four, five, and six. Watch the tape."

Let's grant Gilbert Game 5; there's no dispute he disappeared in that game, possibly because of the unsubstantiated rumors of problems with a teammate. But in Game 6—another game Gilbert cited—against a Celtics team that went to the Finals and outplayed the Lakers—LeBron had 27 points, 19 rebounds, 10 assists, and 3 steals in 46 minutes.

A triple double. If that qualifies as quitting, LeBron should immediately be inducted into the Quitters' Hall of Fame. He's the world's greatest quitter. Retire the trophy.

But whatever. Don't let facts get in the way. LeBron has been labeled a quitter, and there's nothing he can do about it.

Back to Jordan: he quit on his sport—his entire *sport*—during the prime of his career.

One doesn't stick, one defines.

2. LeBron's a traitor: he misled the Cavs and the entire long-suffering city of Cleveland by waiting until a television show to tell the world that he would play in Miami.

Let's look at this a little bit closer. LeBron's destination was the biggest basketball scoop in ten years. Was he going to New York? Miami? Chicago? Would he stay in Cleveland?

Take yourself back to those days and remember how relentless and breathless the reporting became. Every NBA reporter was on this story.

Did he know where he was going? Three days before LeBron announced his decision, Stephen A. Smith told me the people around James had no idea what he was going to do. People *inside* LeBron's inner circle didn't know. And if Stephen A. knew, he would have broken it. There was no value to holding the information. None at all, and as it turned out he broke the news shortly before *The Decision* aired.

And yet the misperception persists: LeBron knew where he was going to play and simply chose not to tell anybody because he wanted to make it hurt Cleveland worse.

Again, this sticks to LeBron like flypaper.

Now, back to Jordan: his longtime trainer, Tim Grover, wrote a book about his days working with Jordan. Before it was published, he told Yahoo! Sports that after the 1992–93 title, Jordan told him, "I'm done. Start preparing me for baseball." And yet it took six months for Jordan to finally get around to informing the Bulls that he was retiring. Back then, it was reported as an abrupt retirement. Tim Grover—and Michael Jordan—knew it was anything but abrupt.

So one guy, by all available evidence, truly didn't know three days before he made his decision and got vilified for it. The other guy made his decision months in advance, withheld the information from his employer and the fans and the media, and yet nobody really questioned it.

It is not arguable that Jordan has been the beneficiary of the single greatest marketing effort in the history of sports. I would contend that LeBron—for his talent level—has been the beneficiary of one of the worst. There is no impenetrable force field around LeBron James. In fact, the only thing surrounding him is a permeable membrane.

With Jordan, nothing gets in.

With LeBron, everything gets in, and nothing gets out.

I asked my
seven-year-old son
to describe what
love is.
"If someone fell off
a cliff and died
and I was sad."
Yep.
Pretty much
nailed it.

Hey, NBA—Let 'Em Play

Simple question: If an 18-year-old technology whiz can graduate from high school and head to Silicon Valley, why can't an 18-year-old basketball whiz graduate from high school and head to the Memphis Grizzlies?

Simple answer: Other than one misguided rule intended to prop up college basketball, there's no reason whatsoever.

College basketball has a problem. Strip college basketball of all the fawning media folks extolling the virtues of every coach. Set aside the mythology built up around March Madness. Forget the emotional connection you might have with your old school, and the pride you feel when it does well. If you view it through clear eyes, you'll see that college basketball occupies a strange place in the American sports landscape.

It's the only major sport where the best people in the sport don't want to be there.

Think about it. The best players are held hostage by the NBA and NCAA to fulfill a bizarre and arbitrary requirement that reeks not only of paternalism but socioeconomic and racial stereotypes.

Football has a mandatory three-year rule, but an 18-year-old football player can't play in the NFL. Physically, emotionally—it's just not possible. Basketball is different. The best 18-year-old basketball players have proven they can compete with the best players in the world. It's a proven fact. They can be among the top 1 percent in the sport at 18 or 19. The examples are on an All Star team near you: Kobe Bryant, Kevin Garnett, Dwight Howard, LeBron James, Dirk Nowitzki.

History doesn't lie.

No other major American sport can say its best players would rather be somewhere else. Despite hockey's labor problems, the best players still want to play in the NHL. The world's best baseball players want to make the big leagues. College football players—with rare exceptions—understand they can't play in the NFL until they've matured physically into grown men.

The best players in college basketball aren't fully invested. They're biding their time, often playing for themselves rather than their teams, keeping one eye on their status for the next NBA draft and one ear bent toward their soon-to-be-agent. This is why college basketball has the bleakest and most vulnerable future of the major sports.

The erosion has been gradual. If someone gains four pounds a year, it's difficult to see. But after ten years, you go back and look at an old photograph and you can't believe it's the same person. That's college basketball: a gradual erosion that's easy to overlook.

Up close, it doesn't look that bad. A lot of the arenas are packed; there's talent and excitement in many small college towns. I get that. But if you pull back a little, you see the erosion. These guys are overcoached and overregulated. They're stifled within the system by practice restrictions and control-freak coaches. One of the most laughable arguments for keeping kids in school comes from those college coaches, who feed the media the line about college being an alleyway to becoming a man and preparing properly for the NBA. We all know where they're coming from—hell, it's their business to make us believe that—but that doesn't mean we can't call it what it is: pure garbage.

It reminds me of this old joke:

Who's the only guy who could hold Michael Jordan under 20?
Dean Smith.

It would be great for everybody if basketball stars were interested in astrophysics or biomechanics or molecular biology, but they aren't. They're interested in basketball the way young prodigy tennis players are interested in tennis and young prodigy entrepreneurs are interested in innovation. At the highest level of commitment, there's not a whole lot of room for anything else.

Is college basketball as an industry really better served by having kids who have absolutely zero interest academically spending two semesters on campus? These guys are no part of the university community except for on the basketball court—how does that make sense? What industry thrives when the best people aren't interested in being there?

It's a bad business model, pure and simple. It's unsustainable.

To put it another way: college basketball has become the apartment complex of big-time American sports, and nobody wants to be in an apartment. Everyone wants to be in a nice condo, or they want to own a house, so there's resentment when you're the guy who's forced to sit in a shabby apartment when you have the means and the aptitude to own a house. It's athletic red-lining.

There's a mythology built up around college basketball, and it all centers on three weeks in March.

Oh, the tournament is so great.
Anything can happen.
Cinderella punches her ticket to the ball.

The tournament—complete with everyone's obsession with their brackets and fifteen seeds beating two seeds and all that— has served to mask many of college basketball's flaws. The regular-season television ratings aren't strong. The quality of play has declined, in part because everyone—coaches, fans, media, the players themselves—knows the best players have one foot out the door. The 2012–13 season, which saw the top ten change drastically week by week, wasn't a fluke. That's the new normal in college hoops.

We hear about all the high school kids who would ruin their lives by declaring for the draft, losing their college eligibility, and never making it big in the NBA. Two things: (1) give them the option to go to college after the draft, the way baseball's draft works; (2) that's why player-personnel guys have jobs—to determine who can and can't play in the league. Let the market work.

There might be washouts, but no more than there are now. Sebastian Telfair, a New York City high school legend, is often put forth as an argument against allowing players to go from high school to the NBA. Telfair was a first-round pick straight out of high school who struggled his first few years before gaining some traction in the league.

He's your example? Really? Telfair makes $1.5 million a year doing what he loves. He's got plenty of money to pursue a college education if he so chooses. And he's a bust? If he's a bust, there's no industry in the world with a better downside. He's the cautionary tale? If he's a cautionary tale, that's not a very scary place.

There isn't some mythical alleyway strewn with failures.

There's a litany of great players who have not only gone directly from high school to the NBA but excelled. Let's break down their attributes. LeBron is one of the smartest basketball players ever to play. Kobe, by any standard, is one of the shrewdest, most competitive, and hardest-working athletes in the past thirty years. Flip Saunders told me Garnett is by far the smartest basketball player he ever coached. Tyson Chandler is one of the most intelligent and socially aware athletes in any sport—just look at his charity work after Hurricane Sandy.

These guys are not desperate dropouts. They're four of the most worldly and composed athletes in any sport. It's unthinkable and demeaning that they would be forced to attend a year of college simply because a group of people with a vested interest in promoting and profiting from the NCAA *as a business* has decided it knows what is best for them.

That's paternalistic and demeaning—not to mention disingenuous. It's based on assumptions involving race and perceived impoverishment. In almost every case, it's older white guys—the media, college coaches, David Stern—telling young black kids what's best for them.

You grow in college, sure—we all understand that. But why are young basketball prodigies treated differently than prodigies in other fields? I had a conversation with Andrew Luck in which he told me professors at Stanford *encourage* geniuses with the next big idea to get out of college and pursue those ideas in the private sector. The idea is more important than the education. For technological geniuses, the private sector is the big leagues. That's why Mark Zuckerberg was smart to leave Harvard and head for Silicon Valley, and the same principle holds for Kevin Durant or Derrick Rose.

They're all prodigies, so why is one exalted for his independence and the others are forced into a paternalistic system that pretends to know what's best for them? The basketball prodigies are patted on the head and told their dreams of going straight from college to the NBA signify an unwillingness to work hard and learn the game. It's racial coding, plain and simple, and it's complete garbage.

There's a belief that these young kids need to be protected from the industry. It's just wrong. The truth is, by the time they're 18 or 19, they know the system inside and out. They know every marketing executive at Adidas and Nike. They know the difference between legitimate agents and street agents. They know how to deal with parasitic coaches.

They know the whole story, and they're smart enough and savvy enough to handle it.

Mike Dunleavy Sr. told me face to face that his son, Mike, left Duke early because he couldn't play against top talent every day in college and he didn't want to risk his earning potential by getting hurt. Doc Rivers's son, Austin, left Duke after his freshman year because every NBA executive knew he was ready to play the game at the highest level and get paid accordingly. These aren't downtrodden, impoverished kids making these decisions. These are the sons of *NBA coaches*. They have access to the best advice in the world, they come from wealthy families, and they know the importance of education. They're not leaving college early because they're desperate; they're leaving early because they're smart.

It's about hopes and dreams and talent, not a blind and ignorant rush to overcome impoverishment.

Shabazz Muhammad is a classic example. He would have been a top-five pick in the 2012 draft; instead the one-year rule put him at UCLA, where he seemed only intermittently interested in the college game. After his final game at Pauley Pavilion, UCLA coach Ben Howland provided a welcome—and rare—hit of honesty. He said Muhammad had played his last game for the Bruins, and that's how it should be. No phony talk about the benefits of college or the purity of the game.

Howland's message was clear: *Muhammad did his time.*

That's all it was: a one-year obligation. What did UCLA get out of it? An okay season, nothing special, certainly nothing close to what the prognosticators expected at the beginning of the season. Muhammad had a good season, certainly nothing transcendent. The lasting memory of his career at UCLA is probably going to be his reaction to teammate Larry Drew's last-second shot to beat Washington. Muhammad looked irritated that he didn't get the last shot, and he wanted no part of his teammates' celebration.

What did Howland get out of it? Fired. The expectations, built largely on the false premise that Muhammad could become a transcendent player, were too big to meet.

To say the sport has the bleakest outlook is not the same as saying it won't survive. Boxing is still around, but it was once huge and has since eroded. Galveston used to be bigger than Houston. JC Penney still exists; it just doesn't have the future of Amazon.com. College basketball isn't going anywhere, but it doesn't have a God-given right to a spot near the top of the pecking order of American sports.

Texas athletic director DeLoss Dodds was recently quoted as saying the sport of college basketball is in shambles. He thinks the sport is being squeezed for publicity because of scheduling. It's competing with the NFL and the NBA, and Dodds wondered if it would help the sport if it moved to a later start.

Let's look at college basketball like a business. What industry thrives when the best employees aren't interested in being there? Let's pretend college basketball is a steakhouse. By Dodds's reasoning, if more people know about the steak in the steakhouse, business will pick up. He's missing the point. It's not a publicity problem; it's a *steak* problem.

If we don't have forgiveness in sports, we may end up with about seven guys left in each league.

Manning Overboard

Robin Williams is in the club within the club, one of those rare entertainers whose audacious talent is viewed reverentially even among other greats. He possesses a brand of comedic skill that can't be crafted, the kind that makes every jaw in the room drop. In his stand-up acts, he walks a tightrope, always seeming to be seconds away from an ugly fall before he lands on a punch line with precision and balance. Watching his career, especially as a solo act, can be as exhilarating for the fan as it must be exhausting for the man who entered our consciousness as Mork.

However, when working with others, Williams doesn't always feel so special.

He and Billy Crystal were making the obligatory movie-hype tour one year when I caught them on a few late-night shows. (The movie they were promoting was one I'd jam my fingers into a hot toaster to avoid seeing, but that's beside the point.) No matter the show, Crystal was suffocated verbally by Williams's relentless sweat-and-spew comedy barrage. It was uncomfortable to watch.

There's no dispute that Williams's career has been remarkable. There's also no dispute that there are times—such as his promo tour with Crystal—when he becomes a victim of his own talent. He overwhelms a room, making it impossible for even a renowned talent to play the sidekick role. There's no sharing the stage, there's only the realization that you need to sit back and allow the hairiest comedian of our generation to erupt. And hope against hope that he lands in a good place.

Peyton Manning always feels the same way to me.

Manning is such an intense, jaw-dropping talent/football

genius/personality/force that sometimes I wonder, is it possible he hinders his success without knowing it?

From college to the pros, coaches have allowed Manning a level of freedom and power they would never otherwise relinquish. Given that, it's inevitable that any team he quarterbacks becomes an extension of what he—one man, Peyton Manning—needs it to be. And what those teams need to be are passing-centric, which creates finesse football teams that are overly reliant on his game-day brilliance. The Colts used his hurry-up offense almost exclusively, and it was Manning directing all of the traffic. He earned the title "Sheriff"—certainly not because he willingly and easily handed over control.

This formula works in the regular season, when Manning-led teams overwhelm less-talented opponents. But his playoff record? Nine wins, eleven losses. Seven times his team lost its playoff opener. Seven one and dones? Seriously? This is Peyton Freaking Manning we're talking about. He's often lost at home, as a favorite, and if you remove the four-game undefeated run to his only Super Bowl win, he's 5-11 as a starting quarterback in the playoffs.

Nobody would argue that he's not a first-ballot Hall of Famer. Of course he is.

Nobody would argue that he wins games others couldn't. Of course he does.

But transcendent talents come with baggage. They aren't unqualified successes. They aren't above criticism. It's not just Manning; Kobe Bryant can take a team to unimagined heights, but he takes so many shots and dominates the ball so thoroughly he can limit the effectiveness of his teammates. Even elite teammates.

Consider this: in Manning's senior year at Tennessee, the Volunteers were an average SEC defense, allowing 22.7 points per game. Even in their biggest win, they slipped past Auburn in the

SEC title game in a shootout, 30-29. The following year, with a much less talented quarterback (Tee Martin), Tennessee not only won the national championship but were in the discussion as the best defensive team in the country, allowing just 14.5 points per game. That team relied on defense as well as a multithreat running game. They were bruising and physical. How could a team be forced to outscore opponents one year and be the nation's most physical team the next? The most dramatic change was Manning's departure to the NFL, and a question needs to be asked: Did Phil Fulmer become so obsessed with Manning's talent that he allowed it to alter the physical nature that Fulmer's past and future teams possessed?

Consider this: despite having Tony Dungy, one of the NFL's leading defensive minds, as a head coach for a decade, not one of the Colts' defenses were ever considered physically elite. From Manning's rookie year (1998) to the final year he played for the Colts (2010), Indianapolis had a defense ranked in the top ten in yards allowed just twice. In seven of Manning's Indy years, the Colts' defense resided in the bottom half of the NFL. It's even harder to fathom when you consider then-Colts president Bill Polian is one of the league's shrewdest talent evaluators. Did he have an eye for offensive talent only? How did a six-time league executive of the year not find a way to land more defensive studs?

Toughness and physicality are not built on Sundays. Instead, they're created during the week, during practice. How can a team possibly develop a physical culture when week-to-week preparation is dominated by mastering Manning's "Rain Man" aerial wizardry?

Similarly, how can you create a movie around Robin Williams without allowing him to ad lib? Isn't the organic evolution of his comedic Zen the reason you cast him in the first place?

Transcendent talent comes with baggage. *Give, take. Push, pull.* You make concessions when you cast Peyton Manning as your quarterback. He's going to eat a lot of scenery.

Of the top ten quarterbacks of the past forty years, none but Manning was saddled with perennially mediocre defenses. Marino wasn't. Aikman wasn't. Elway wasn't. Brady wasn't. Bradshaw wasn't. Montana wasn't. Manning was—with one of the best defensive minds as a head coach and an equally respected general manager. Was he just the unluckiest great quarterback ever?

Does Peyton bear some responsibility? When your personality and talent is so all-consuming, there has to be some linkage, right?

Bill Polian came on my radio show in 2012, and I cornered him with my theory. I asked him whether Manning's talent, maybe superior to any quarterback in history, actually worked to the detriment of his team's defenses.

He smiled at me and said, "Right church, wrong pew."

Translation: You're close, but not quite, kid.

Once the Colts landed Manning, Polian told me, they knew they had to build the team a certain way. Manning would not only lead the team to many, many wins, but over the course of those games his team would have some serious leads. Logical, right? The Colts would routinely be ahead in games, and that meant opposing teams would be forced to throw the ball to catch up.

As a result, Polian had a specific emphasis: pass rushers, and linebackers who could run and cover tight ends or backs in the flat.

In essence, Manning's presence requires his teams to be built a certain way. The defense can't be overly reliant on stopping the run, and the offense can't be overly reliant on running the ball.

In the NFL, you can't be all things to all people. You have

to constantly juggle a tight salary cap and a limited roster that is under the constant strain of nonstop injuries. Polian had to make choices. With Manning calling the shots, the choices were simple: pass—and stop the pass—first.

These are the same kinds of choices studios, directors, and writers have to make. Who works well with a particular movie star? How do the bit players make the star better without getting in his way? How much leeway will the megatalent have to ad lib and improvise?

Fans—and probably a vast majority of the media—have been conditioned to believe that unique, transcendent talent is a magic elixir. But talent also creates ancillary problems that ancillary people—studio heads, directors, coaches, general managers—have to solve in order to accommodate the talent.

When XM/Sirius radio was created, it snagged radio superstar Howard Stern. It was a decision that created a trickle-down effect. Now that we've got Howard, should we build our entire brand around him? The danger is obvious: if the superstar leaves, the identity walks out the door with him. It's a thin and perilous line, one walked by corporations and teams alike.

In the NFL, rosters are smaller than they are in college. Offensive and defensive players are forced to practice together. Isn't it reasonable to assume that a quarterback as gifted as Manning—running an offense predicated almost entirely on those gifts—would be given uncommon freedom to improvise? Wouldn't some level of control have to be surrendered to allow uncommon talent to flourish? You would be wasting him otherwise, in much the same way you'd be wasting Robin Williams by forcing him to adhere to someone else's script.

It's the paradox of greatness, and it creates the greatest compliment and the rarest criticism:

Dear Peyton and Robin,

Sometimes you were just too talented for your own good.

Love,
Colin

**Love your life,
like your sports.**

Pace Yourself

There's no question racism exists in sports. We can talk around it and write around it. We can call it something else and pretend it doesn't exist. Or, we can take a different approach: call it exactly what it is and deal with it.

The NBA occupies a unique place in the American sports landscape. Its players don't wear masks or caps or cover their arms with sleeves. Whether they're playing or sitting on the bench, their proximity to the fans is far closer than any other sport.

This means the crowd—the mostly white, mostly corporate crowd—gets an up-close look at these large, muscular black athletes. They see their faces and their tats and their sweat. Up close. And I think it makes many in the mostly white, mostly corporate crowd uncomfortable.

Race has always been an undercurrent in the NBA, far more than in any other sport. David Stern instituted a dress code in 2005 and it immediately became a racial issue. If Bud Selig or Roger Goodell or the commissioner of the MLS instituted a dress code, race never would have been mentioned. In the NBA, when Stern decided his mostly corporate crowd might be turned off by 'do rags and sunglasses inside and at night, race was front and center.

The NFL is 67 percent African-American; the NBA, 77 percent. It might not seem like a huge difference, until you realize the vast majority of stars in the NBA are black while the biggest names in the NFL, for the most part, are quarterbacks. And quarterbacks are historically white.

But the most illuminating laboratory for the issue of race in the NBA takes us to Indianapolis, where a curious and ongoing experiment seems to be taking place: the Pacers can't draw fans, despite having an elite team that plays in an elite arena in a city whose sleepiness is so well known it's nicknamed Naptown.

It's one of the great mysteries in sports. A team that took Miami to seven games in the Eastern Conference Finals playing the NBA's best defense and leading the league in rebounding in the self-proclaimed sacred temple of hard-nosed basketball ranked twenty-fifth in attendance. They were outdrawn by the Timberwolves, Cavaliers, and Suns. Seriously, the *Suns*?

When the ownership group that successfully fought to keep the Kings in Sacramento were in the final stages of negotiations, it agreed to decline the NBA's revenue-sharing money. Commonly known as the Ailing Team Fund, the revenue sharing is the NBA's welfare fund, allowing small-money, small-market teams to benefit from the huge profits accumulated by their big-money, big-market brethren.

The decision of the Kings' owners was followed by a truly astounding revelation. An economist at the University of California, Irvine, who studies the NBA, reported that just two teams in the league benefited from the Ailing Team Fund more than the Kings.

One of those teams was the Memphis Grizzlies.

The other was the Indiana Pacers.

On the surface, it seems outrageous. A perennial playoff team in a two-team pro market in the mythical capital of basketball can't draw flies. In fact, just for fun I checked on Stubhub in the middle of the 2012–13 season for tickets to a Pacers home game against the Clippers. On the day of the game, I discovered I could buy a ticket to the game between two of the best teams in the league for $2.95. That's less than the cost of most espresso drinks.

Here's my take: the Pacers are still paying the price for the Malice in the Palace, an incident that took place in 2004 in Detroit.

Not Indianapolis—Detroit. That night lingers in Indianapolis like a bad smell, even after nearly a decade and when the Pacers had a roster full of enigmatic players such as Ron Artest and Stephen Jackson.

It doesn't matter that the current version of the Pacers bears no resemblance to that one. It doesn't matter that the brawl happened nine years ago or that it was *a Pistons home game.* It doesn't matter that Ron Artest is not only long gone but has a whole new name. Three of them, to be exact.

Let's call this a case of residual racism. Not necessarily overt racism, but racism that drifted through the franchise like a virus in the arena's circulation system. Many people swore off the NBA and the Pacers after the Malice in the Palace. We can see the lingering effects to this day, in the poor attendance and surprisingly bad business fortunes of one of the most entertaining, successful franchises in the NBA.

This metaphorical virus was contracted and spread by a very small number of black athletes. In the NBA, unlike any other professional American sport, the actions of a few speak loudly for all the players. They all get lumped together, no matter how unfair or downright stupid it might seem.

During roughly the same time span since the Malice at the Palace, the Indianapolis Colts had twenty-three arrests. Doesn't matter—people still pay big money to fill Lucas Oil Stadium every time the Colts play. It didn't hurt that their star of stars, Peyton Manning, was a white quarterback who looked like he could have lived down the block from a large majority of the season-ticket holders. The Colts, however, were in the upper echelon of NFL teams when it came to arrests during the 2000s. There're no long-term repercussions, though. There aren't even short-term repercussions—it's the NFL, not the NBA. Fans don't see the faces or the tats or sit close enough to feel the heat coming off their bodies. The NFL is detached, impersonal, a bunch of pads running into each other for entertainment and gambling purposes.

Here's another stat: the NFL had twenty-seven arrests in twenty-three weeks—twenty-three *weeks*—in the off-season following the 2012–13 season. That's more than an arrest a week. But it doesn't stick to the NFL. They don't lose advertisers, we don't judge them, we don't refuse to show up to local games. Nobody in Indianapolis seems to say, "I'm not going to watch the Colts this weekend because several published reports have linked Marvin Harrison to the 2008 murder of a man named Dwight Dixon in Philadelphia." No, because what's happening with the Pacers is almost unheard of in American sports. They're winning in a boring two-team-market town and nobody is going to the games.

Outdrawn by the T-Wolves.

Outdrawn by the Suns.

The *Suns*?

Yes, the Suns.

Have you *seen* the Suns?

Permit me this tangent: a study of 3,500 NBA players showed that each one plays for 2.5 teams over the course of his career. Players who average more than thirty minutes per game during their careers—star or high-end players—play for an average of 2.99 teams. Even star players like Patrick Ewing and Karl Malone and Michael Jordan don't end their careers in the same uniform they wore their rookie years. Everybody gets traded in the NBA, but it's rarely on players' terms.

With this routine changing of uniforms, why were so many people outraged by LeBron James leaving Cleveland? Was it because a black player—on *his* terms—chose his destination? The words of Cavaliers owner Dan Gilbert were telling. He called it "cowardly betrayal," "selfish," a "shocking act of disloyalty," a "heartless and callous action." It reads like a vicious, crazed Zagat entry.

But before we crucify LeBron, can it be duly noted that in seven years in Cleveland they—meaning Gilbert—didn't provide him with another all-star–caliber player? And can it be noted, for the record, that James was . . . you know . . . a *free* agent?

I believe part of the backlash against LeBron relates to the aftereffects from the Malice in the Palace. It's the fear of the threatening black man. LeBron is big, he's strong, he's got tats, he scowls. I'm not saying that's all of it, but that's part of it. I'm not saying we love all white athletes. I'm not saying we dislike or fear all black athletes. But when you look at Dan Gilbert and you look at the Indiana Pacers and you look at the way we hold NBA players accountable for off-field indiscretions, the conclusion is indisputable: it's a much, *much* harsher standard than you find anywhere else. If Charlie Sheen acts like a douche bag, it doesn't speak for all Caucasians. When Josh Brent got a DUI and killed his friend, it didn't speak for every NFL player. Hell, it didn't even speak for every Dallas Cowboy. It simply doesn't stick. But if Latrell Sprewell chokes a coach, or Ron Artest throws a punch, it seems to speak in some broad sense for all African-American NBA players.

(It's interesting to note that Kevin Durant—marketed across the country as nonthreatening and friendly and likable, for good reason—has a ton of tats. The difference? He's placed them strategically inside his uniform shell. They're there, but you just don't see them, therefore he's palatable to the ticket-buying segment of corporate white America.)

I've been talking about sports professionally for more than twenty years, and the word *thug* on my Twitter account and e-mails—especially e-mails—gets used routinely to label NBA players. The occurrence of this one word in reference to NBA players far exceeds that of any other sport. It's not even close. Former NBA star and current ESPN commentator Jalen Rose once told me that players always laugh at NBA fights. He told me, "Man, we don't wear hats and we don't wear helmets. Our face is our moneymaker. Nobody wants to take a punch in the NBA." If you watch most NBA "fights," you can see Rose's words in action. Guys square off and wait for someone to pull them apart. And yet, somehow, no sport has more athletes called *thug*.

Can we be honest? It's racial coding.

John Daly, with a private life that would singe Keith Richards's eyebrows, is a good ol' boy.

Allen Iverson? Thug.

And the Pacers are still paying the price for the actions of a few black athletes. With a winning team in one of the less energized cities in America—Naptown, remember—they simply can't draw.

I present, as a counterpoint, the city of Portland, Oregon. The Blazers sell out, even though they play in a worse arena with a worse team. The Blazers sell out, even though Portland is the No. 1 cycling city in the country, is an exceptional culinary town, is located one hour from the beach, and is one of the few U.S. cities close to year-round mountain skiing. The Blazers sell out, even though a far higher portion of the Portland population is earthy and eccentric, two qualities that aren't automatically associated with rabid sports fans. The Blazers sell out, even though the franchise went through the better part of a decade being called "The Jail Blazers" because of the criminal behavior of several of its players— behavior far worse than anything the Pacers did in Detroit.

I can hear you out there: *Colin, it's the economy.* Really? Is that why Portland is in the top ten in NBA attendance and home television ratings? Is it the economy? As of December 2012, Indiana had

8 percent unemployment. Oregon? Eight percent unemployment. The economy argument doesn't hold water.

Maybe voting patterns provide a more incisive look. Portland is progressive, tolerant, tech-embracing. Indianapolis is the most conservative city in America with a population above 500,000. There has to be something, right? Because on the surface, it makes no sense. The Pacers, tops in the league in rebounding, defense, and effort, are the perfect team for Hoosierville. And yet . . .

There's more empirical evidence, courtesy of the Harris poll. According to them, the NFL is much bigger than college football, the NHL is much bigger than college hockey, and MLB is much bigger than college baseball. But the difference between the NBA and college basketball? Slim. Considering the quality of play in college basketball has been gradually sliding for years, why is college basketball almost as popular as the NBA?

Part of it is simply this: the NBA is the league with black stars. It doesn't do well in TV ratings in rural communities. It does well in ethnic communities: Atlanta, Houston, New York, Miami, Chicago, Dallas. Race plays a role. The evidence is undeniable.

Mike Lupica once wrote that the NBA is the only sport where the fans don't really like the players. Buzz Bissinger, noted author of *Friday Night Lights,* created a minor shitstorm at the NBA All Star Weekend in Los Angeles in 2010 when he attributed the NBA's lack of popularity to a dearth of American-born white stars.

Was Bissinger just stirring up trouble? Looking for attention? I'm not so sure. On my flight home from that All Star Weekend in Los Angeles, I sat next to the marketing director for an NBA franchise. I asked him about the team's first-round pick in the previous year's draft. He grimaced and shook his head. This man who is in charge of selling his team to its fan base said he wished his team had picked a certain college guard instead.

When I asked him why, he looked me dead in the eye and said, "We could really use a white guard to market to our fans."

His tone was direct and matter-of-fact. I got the impression he was left with no choice but to acknowledge a problem he wished didn't exist.

Proximity to greatness doesn't equal greatness. Rubbing elbows with it doesn't rub off.

Greatness comes from deep within people. It's part drive and part focus. To maintain it also takes the same drive and commitment.

And just forget about trying to be great at two things. It almost never happens.

Remember how bad a fit Magic Johnson was briefly as the Lakers' head coach? It doesn't even seem possible. He learned from Pat Riley and Phil Jackson and still seemed lost? This was a guy with an innate feel for the game of basketball but in a huddle wearing a tie? It just didn't feel right and Magic knew it instantly.

Back in the early 1990s the Washington Huskies were a top ten college football powerhouse. The man who built their program, Don James, retired abruptly. They gave the job to his longtime assistant, Jim Lambright. He stood next to James for around twenty years. They were in the same meeting rooms. Had a constant football dialogue for two decades. Yet just a few years after taking over my favorite team of all time, it dissolved back into a mediocre program.

Proximity to greatness doesn't equal greatness.

Instead of hiring stars that seem like perfect fits for jobs, why not go find the next star?

Just because people are close to brilliance or talent doesn't mean they have it.

Otherwise, you wouldn't have so many loser kids from successful parents. It's about the drive and focus, not the proximity.

A-Rod using performance-enhancing drugs is similar to George Clooney getting plastic surgery. It just feels greedy.

Pick Your Poison

When Robert Griffin III was named the 2012 NFL Rookie of the Year, there wasn't even a ripple of protest in the sports world. Twitter didn't erupt, or even bubble, with cries of injustice. RGIII won, in a landslide, beating out Andrew Luck, and that was simply how it was supposed to be.

But was it really that obvious? Was the argument for Griffin over Luck really so convincing it didn't even merit a spirited conversation? I once casually mentioned that Thursday is my favorite day of the week, and I lost more than 2,500 Twitter followers by the end of the next day. Misspell a word on Twitter and see how many people mock your education. Pick a side in a movie debate—say you like *The Hangover* better than *The Wedding Crashers*—and you might earn yourself a death threat.

And yet, Griffin over Luck didn't even bump the needle. Not even a little bit. Not even in Indianapolis.

Why? Why did the vote—29 of 50 first-place votes went to Griffin—seem so anticlimactic? There's no dispute that Luck did more with substantially less, and that he clobbered Griffin in nearly every single relevant statistical category.

Except one: interceptions.

Luck had 18; Griffin, 5.

Voters couldn't bend their minds around that one statistic, a statistic so widely misunderstood that it shouldn't be used as a barometer of much of anything at all. But because of it, Luck was deemed—by a wide margin—to be the second-best rookie in the NFL.

Here's the problem: we have absolutely no idea what to make of an interception. With all the advancements in the analytics of sports, all the next-level statistics and advanced metrics, all of the NFL's ability to seamlessly link technology to its sport, the interception remains tied to an old-fashioned concept of good vs. evil.

Interceptions are bad. All of them. Can't win with them and can't lose without them. They're a one-size-fits-all statistic. The quarterback who throws more of them is worse than the quarterback who throws fewer of them. End of story.

In this day and age, it's amazing that we still think this way.

Let's remember how Luck ended up in Indianapolis. The Colts got the No. 1 pick in the draft because they earned it. They earned it because they were terrible, the worst team in the league in 2011 by a wide margin. They weren't just bad at quarterback; they were bad all over. When they drafted Luck, that didn't change anything beside the quarterback position. The personnel surrounding Luck was bad during his rookie year, too.

Luck played behind one of the worst offensive lines in the league. His running game was almost nonexistent. He had one good veteran receiver, Reggie Wayne, but receivers alone don't have much impact. We promote them and are amazed by their athletic abilities, but they are wholly dependent on the people around them. Calvin Johnson is the league's most gifted receiver—Detroit finished last in its division. Larry Fitzgerald and DeSean Jackson finished last, too. Success in the NFL starts with the protection of the number one asset, the quarterback. Green Bay is a perfect case in point: the league's best quarterback, Aaron Rodgers, has struggled to win playoff games after winning the Super Bowl for one reason—his offensive line is dreadful.

And it's not nearly as bad as the one that lined up in front of Andrew Luck.

Luck spent a season running for his life behind a porous offensive line and getting little to no help from a running game. RGIII spent a season being protected by one of the league's best offensive lines, one that helped an unheralded rookie running back, Alfred Morris, run for more than 1,600 yards. Griffin's game plans were devised by Mike Shanahan, one of the most respected offensive minds in the game, while Luck had an interim head coach, Bruce Arians.

A poor offensive line, a nonexistent running game, and an interim head coach—can you think of a worse situation for a rookie starting quarterback?

And yet take a look at the statistics: Luck was forced to throw 230 times more than RGIII and completed 80 more; he threw for almost 1,200 more yards, had more touchdown passes, more yards per game, more yards per completion, and 600 more all-purpose yards.

He was also more durable, and it's worth noting that availability is the best way to judge ability. RGIII was unable to finish three games because of injury.

Throughout the season, ESPN's sharpest analysts provided keen insight into the reasons behind RGIII's lack of interceptions. He was running a simpler offense and asked to take fewer chances. He made fewer—and easier—reads downfield.

One of the greatest compliments a coach can pay a young quarterback is to increase the amount of offense he's *allowed* to run. The playbook grows with preparation and readiness. Luck is a Stanford graduate who played four years in a pro-style offense. Arians told me Luck was so brilliant he was able to open up the entire playbook by the end of the preseason.

RGIII is obviously a smart kid as well, but his transition was far different. Baylor ran a spread offense during Griffin's three seasons there (he missed one with an injury) and was given an offense with limited options—mostly a slicker version of the one he ran in college—to make his rookie year easier.

They're both great young quarterbacks who could be the faces of the league for the next decade, but the difference in responsibility they were given is not insignificant. If you're a parent of two kids, you don't love one more than the other, but if you send them both to the amusement park, you're going to pick one of them to hold the money.

You love 'em both.

Both good kids.

One holds the money.

So let's review the who-holds-the-money question as it pertains to Luck and Griffin:

Better surrounding talent:	RGIII.
Better offensive line:	RGIII.
Better running game:	RGIII.
Better, more experienced head coach:	RGIII.
Better production:	Luck.

Griffin's better completion percentage is a by-product of an offense that relied on safer, easier throws. He had better quarterback rating, but that isn't the be-all, end-all stat some would like you to believe it is. For one thing, John Elway's QBR is sixty-third all-time, behind Chad Pennington, Jeff Garcia, Shaun Hill, Marc Bulger, Brad Johnson, Neil O'Donnell, and Dave Krieg. In many ways, the quarterback rating has all the accuracy of an online hotel review.

This takes us on our long and winding path back to the "dreaded" interception, another statistic that tells you roughly as much about quarterbacking as someone's opinion of the color of a bedspread tells you about the Ritz-Carlton.

This isn't a mystery within the game. Phil Simms loves to tell stories about his former boss, Bill Parcells, and the gruff advice he gave his quarterback. Before one game, Parcells told Simms, "If you don't throw two interceptions today, I'm going to be pissed." Parcells, the only coach in NFL history to lead four different teams to the playoffs, understood that passivity was the enemy of the quarterback. He knew that Simms needed to get out of his comfort zone, be aggressive, and take chances downfield in order for the Giants to succeed. He knew that big games are often won by off-the-script plays made downfield, often in traffic, and those plays aren't made by dumping the ball off to a back in the flat.

Parcells, whose coaching tree includes Tom Coughlin, Sean Payton, and Bill Belichick, once scolded Simms at practice for dropping the ball off to a running back.

"Were you worried it would hurt your completion percentage?" he yelled.

Parcells's lack of fear is borne out by recent history. Of the last eight Super Bowl–winning quarterbacks, seven threw a significant number of interceptions. Eli Manning has won two Super Bowls—he has averaged almost 17 picks his first eight years in the league and threw 23 touchdowns and 20 picks during his first Super Bowl year. Ben Roethlisberger, a known risk-taker, has also won two of those Super Bowls—he had 17 touchdowns and 15 interceptions the only year he played all sixteen games. The great Peyton Manning has had eight years with at least 15 interceptions—one with 28.

Need more? Brett Favre is the all-time leader in interceptions thrown. Joe Namath threw more picks than touchdowns in his career.

Since interceptions are so bad, how in the world do these guys keep winning?

How is it even possible?

Well, it's possible because nobody has ever cared enough—or

taken the time—to analyze the interception. It's possible because the NFL's marketing and hype has led us to accept the idea that the league is an aerial circus, where the last team with the ball wins and every change of possession can swing the outcome of a game. The facts—NFL teams average roughly twelve possessions per game and score on fewer than four of them—don't back up the PR campaign.

Unlike errors in baseball or turnovers in basketball—mistakes that are irrefutably bad—interceptions are not created equal. I believe they fall into two distinct categories:

A. *"Uh-oh, that's going to leave a mark, and Coach is going to be pissed":* These are the interceptions that fall into two subcategories—they are either taken back for touchdowns or occur in the red zone or deep enough in your own territory to nullify potential points.

B. *"No big deal—he just saved our punter a jog onto the field":* These are the interceptions that take place between the 35-yard lines.

Interceptions are a complex business. There are several variables to consider: where they are thrown from, where they are caught, and where they are returned to. Taking all of these factors into consideration, Luck's eighteen interceptions don't look so bad. In fact, just half—only nine—fall into Category A.

This was the big black mark on Luck's season? *This* was the defining difference between him and RGIII? Are you kidding me?

Nine damaging interceptions changed our perception of Andrew Luck?

Look, I understand all of RGIII's great qualities. He's

incredibly charismatic, an exciting player with a great personality. I know he played for a historically relevant franchise and had a hell of a rookie season.

I also know Andrew Luck threw the ball 627 times—more than Dan Marino or John Elway were ever asked to throw in a season—behind an offensive line with more holes than Oliver Stone's version of the JFK assassination. He was aided by a running game so weak, linebackers often dropped into coverage immediately with the snap of the ball. He was led by an interim head coach whose arsenal of weapons consisted of wide receiver Reggie Wayne and a bunch of rookies.

And *interceptions* cost him the Rookie of the Year award?

Clearly, we need a new way of evaluating interceptions.

The Luck vs. Griffin debate underscores that larger point. For as much as we obsess on the NFL, for as much as we bet on it and analyze it and fret over our fantasy teams, interceptions have fallen through the cracks. We, and I include myself, haven't found a way to see anything other than a black number on a white page.

Someday—maybe someday soon—we'll come to a better and more evolved understanding of the interception. We won't toss them all into the same category. As analytics progress, we'll come to understand the nuances.

But for now, the interception is understood about as well as marijuana was in the 1940s.

It makes you go blind. Or worse.

Reefer Madness, meet *Interception Madness.*

But maybe there's hope: if we follow the same evolutionary process, someday we'll realize NFL teams can use interceptions for actual benefits as well.

How you do
under pressure
always reveals
who you really are
as a person.
When you're in
dire straits,
the way you act
when your son
strikes out in a
big game on a bad
call on strike three
determines who
you really are.

Daddy Dearest

About five years ago, I experienced a sudden, unexpected, life-altering event.

I got old.

Fast.

On Saturday night, I was vibrant, alive, seeking new challenges. By Sunday morning, I was craving sliced tomatoes, looking forward to *Meet the Press*, and wondering where I put my glasses.

Things hurt now. I'm told they're called ligaments.

However, there are benefits that come with drifting into your midforties. The biggest one? Perspective. You start looking at life and—in my case—sports differently in middle age. There's very little that surprises me anymore. A younger person might be shocked or outraged by what an athlete does either on the field or off, but I'm the one off in the corner, shrugging. It's just another day at the office, and whatever that guy did is just another in a series of incidents that have taken place on the corner of Bad Temper Avenue and Lousy Judgment Street.

After forty years of watching sports and twenty-five years of covering it, I'd say I'm surprised about once a decade.

Magic Johnson's HIV announcement tops the list. O.J. Simpson's car chase was a jaw-dropper. And oh yeah—Andre Agassi did meth. I didn't see that one coming.

But how anyone can be regularly surprised by the intersection of sports and drugs, sports and sex, or sports and gambling is beyond me. Fame, youth, testosterone, and massive quantities of disposable income create a toxic jambalaya.

The ugly side of sports doesn't diminish my enjoyment. I don't base my opinion of an actor's work on the most sordid details of his personal life. They're performers, and some are eccentric. Most have surrendered some vital part of their life to achieve greatness in the arts, and athletes are no different. Once you realize that athletes are nothing more than tall, fast, and strong entertainers, you begin to expect the flaws. It's just another layer of who they are.

Athletes have it rougher than other entertainers, though. Far rougher. They wear jerseys, and those jerseys have the names of cities across the front. This creates a false civic connection between fans and athletes. Athletes don't represent the residents of their cities any more than a theater troupe does. The misbehavior of a St. Louis athlete who grew up in Florida and went to college in Alabama has no linkage whatsoever with the people of St. Louis.

Imagine this conversation:

WIFE: Honey, I'm really looking forward to our trip to San Diego to see the Johnsons.

HUSBAND: Yeah, about that . . . I've been meaning to tell you that the Chargers' tight end got a DUI last night so I don't think we can hang out with the Johnsons anymore. I used to enjoy their company, but now I see they're really irresponsible.

Problems off the field or off the court are a logical offshoot of unbalanced lives. To be great at anything, you've generally had to sacrifice something else. Give and take, you know? It's the same reason there aren't many top scientists with a killer jump shot.

I give jocks a lot of leeway on my show. I'm more understanding of their mistakes because I see them from a wider angle. Besides, experience has taught me to expect them.

However (and this is a big *however*), there are two specific positions in sports—point guard and quarterback—that bring out the inflexible, ligament-stressed old man in me. Not coincidentally, this is the one topic that brings me the most heat.

At times, it can feel like a blast furnace.

Quarterback and point guard, the two most important leadership positions in sports. If you play one of those two positions, I will judge you and my judgment can be harsh. Sometimes I think I shouldn't be as harsh, but then I return to the same question: Do you believe general managers and owners aren't making those exact same judgments?

These are big-money businesses we're talking about here, and a blown pick at the top of the draft at one of these two vital positions can set a franchise back several years. You can't overstate the importance of the quarterback and point guard. They're the foundation for subsequent draft picks. They need to deal with crises more regularly than any other position and they have to be the ones to stabilize locker rooms during unsettled times.

When people ask me, "How can you possibly ask those questions?" I have a quick response: "How can you *not*?"

I want to know some things about the guys who are going to be entrusted with running my franchise. What's your family background? Is it stable? Was there a father figure around?

There is a direct correlation between childhood family upheaval and disruption in adult lives. Are you telling me I can't ask about that?

I want to know about your friends. Who do you surround yourself with? Unlike the average, 57-year-old American millionaire, you're going to get rich at an early age. Will sudden wealth change you?

Here's the deal: if I run the front office of a major American franchise, I don't have time for you to grow up. Dr. Phil's not on the payroll, so you need to arrive prepackaged and ready to lead.

You have roughly eight years of physical prime to make a ton of money and win a lot of games. My fate is directly connected to yours, so let me put this as delicately as I can:

Do you have your shit together *today*?

If you don't want the added burden that comes with answering those questions, change positions. Play shooting guard. Be a tight end or a safety.

I know you have problems in your past. I know none of it is your fault. But we're dealing with two unavoidable truths: we have a business to run and you have a career to start. Let's say we combine those two and turn this into a happy marriage from Day One?

Dolphins general manager Jeff Ireland was viciously attacked in the media for asking Dez Bryant if his mother was a prostitute. It was a ridiculous question, but not in the way you might think. To me, it was a ridiculous question because Dez Bryant is a wide receiver. The question was irrelevant because Bryant doesn't play a leadership position.

If Dez Bryant was a quarterback, I might have asked the same question.

I'm not a child-development expert but—to my knowledge, anyway—neither is any NFL or NBA general manager or person-nel director. They need answers, though, and they need to ask the kinds of questions that get them as close as possible to the truth. The NFL and NBA have salary caps, so a GM can't just buy his way out of a terrible mistake.

If I'm a general manager, I'm going to be extremely interested in your life from the time you were 4 till you were 16, or whenever you burst into the public consciousness. Those years could tell me which way you're headed and how long it will take to get there. I need to ask questions. I need to make judgments.

If you don't like it, or if you can't handle it—hey, that probably tells me all I need to know.

There's some urgency here. You're an athlete, not a politician. You don't have the kind of shelf life that will allow you to reinvent yourself in your early forties to atone for earlier stumbles. You're not an academic who might seek therapy to unravel the meaning of all of your preteen obstacles.

Again: Are you ready to lead *today*?

Bobby Beathard, former GM of the Chargers, saw his legacy turn to scorched earth after drafting Ryan Leaf. In retrospect, don't you think Beathard would have liked to know that Leaf was considered to be a bully by many in his small Montana hometown? Do you think it would have altered Beathard's opinion had he known that Leaf had once been ejected from a Little League game?

Couldn't a reasonable person see an early warning sign in Vince Young's past, which included a mostly absentee father who had spent time in prison for burglary? Young, a chronic NFL underachiever like Leaf, had a career marked by several regrettable choices. As a pro, he quickly became friends with Pac Man Jones, whose own father was killed in a robbery.

The NFL has used the Wonderlic Cognitive Test for more than two decades to determine the learning and problem-solving capabilities of its draftees. What's the one position that concerns team executives the most? Quarterback, by far. In fact, outside of that one position test scores are rarely revealed or discussed. Frankly, other positions don't matter as much and don't demand the same kind of scrutiny in terms of IQ, maturity, and quick decision making.

I met then-Duke point guard Kyrie Irving on my radio show, and within ninety seconds it was crystal clear to me that he would not only be an excellent player but the kind of person who could maintain a healthy image off the court. He was sharp, assertive, and confident. He looked me straight in the eye. When I said he looked frail—something I said both on and off the air—he responded with a clever verbal jab.

Irving had no posse and no need for one. He's a leader and his own man, something you could feel in his presence. And sure enough, his background meshed nicely with his aura: he was born in Australia, his father played basketball internationally, and he grew up in a solid, suburban neighborhood in West Orange, New Jersey.

Solid family.

Solid kid.

It's a universal equation.

I felt the same way meeting each of the three remarkable quarterbacks who played their rookie years in 2012: Andrew Luck of the Colts, Russell Wilson of the Seahawks, and Robert Griffin III of the Redskins. I knew they were each talented football play-ers, but upon meeting them I was struck by the consistent qualities they exhibited. Each one made strong eye contact, had confident—but not arrogant—body language, and showed a sense I can only describe inarticulately as *with-it-ness*. Arm strength goes only so far; I was blown away by the poise and personality of each young man. These guys are going to be asked to lead groups of alpha males for the next decade, and Central Casting couldn't have come up with better men for the job.

Not surprisingly, all three come from rock-solid families.

If you work in sports long enough, you can spot the success stories and bankruptcies years before they arrive. You don't need to be a sociologist—just pay attention. I don't need to be a marriage counselor to know a bad marriage when I see one.

Past performance absolutely can predict future results.

Right about now, I have a pretty good idea what you're thinking: *Isn't he going to mention John Wall?*

I received massive amounts of criticism for calling out the Wizards' then-rookie point guard one day on the air. I was charged with being everything from insensitive to racist. I think the context of my criticism got lost amid the noise.

After being introduced at his first NBA home game, Wall launched into a thirty-second dance known as "The Dougie." This was outrageous to me, and I said so on the air. Maybe ten years into a career—with a few championships to your name—then *maybe* I could stomach an abbreviated version of what Wall did. But can you imagine anyone, in their first day of work, showboating into the office? It was such an incredible lapse of basic common sense and judgment that I slammed Wall for his immaturity and idiocy.

I don't take any of it back. That one incident told me all I need to know about John Wall.

He just doesn't get it.

He is a huge talent, but leadership and talent are two differ-ent things. Wall, to this point, lacks the fundamental leadership qualities, the overall *with-it-ness* that I see in RGIII and Luck and Irving.

Had I left my observations there, I probably wouldn't have received much criticism. But I want to know why some guys pos-sess these qualities and others don't. I want to look into back-grounds and mentalities to find trends and truths.

Here's what I found: Overwhelmingly, leadership starts at home. Sure enough, Wall grew up in a broken family. His father was incarcerated and released from prison around the time John turned eight. Through no fault of his own—let me repeat that, *through no fault of his own*—Wall is a kid who dealt with baggage and instability that I wouldn't wish on anyone.

And even though it's not his fault, it's part of the package he brings to the NBA.

There's no formula for success in professional sports. I'm not about to say that *solid family + athletic talent = All Star.* Still, it doesn't hurt to play the percentages, and the percentages say a good family and a less chaotic background sets the stage for success in the rest of your life. This goes double for those in leadership positions. Make a list of great leaders in sports; most come from stable families with strong fathers.

John Elway. Derek Jeter. Magic Johnson. Tom Brady. Peyton and Eli Manning. Michael Jordan. Bill Belichick.

Now turn it around and make a list of some of the most troubled and disruptive athletes in sports: Dennis Rodman. Pac Man Jones. Milton Bradley. Chris "Bird Man" Andersen. Terrell Owens. Metta World Peace.

What do they have in common? Predictably unstable backgrounds.

Chaos doesn't inhibit talent—in some cases, it ignites it—but it absolutely can become a roadblock to leadership, which is an essential quality for great quarterbacks and point guards.

The people who called me unfair or racist also criticized me for playing the role of radio sociologist. Look, this isn't that hard. The evidence is out there, as close as a few keystrokes on the Internet.

There's a bigger issue at play here: Are we supposed to refrain from criticizing young athletes for fear of being labeled? Should we just close our eyes and pretend their actions are redeemable without any intervention or acknowledgment? Should we just let all the bankruptcy numbers rise and the string of broken lives continue?

Or do we owe these talented young men guidance, even if it comes in the form of harsh words and occasional criticism?

In the *International Review for the Sociology of Sport,* Joshua Dubrow and Jimi Adams studied the backgrounds of NBA players for a ten-year period (1994–2004). Among their findings, they write, "The intersection of race, class and family structure presents unequal pathways into the league." They discovered that a white athlete raised in a non–two-parent family was 33 percent less likely to make the pros, while the number among African-American families was 18 percent. Doesn't it stand to reason that once in the NBA, the experience from those backgrounds would either assist or inhibit? Of course it does. We can't leave our experiences behind just because we landed a good job or make a lot of money or suddenly have more friends than we can count.

Translation: dads matter—a lot; background matters—a lot.

And when it comes to point guards and quarterbacks, it's crucial. It's a topic that needs to be part of any honest discussion of sports.

I've made my judgment on Irving and Wall: Irving will rise to a higher level. It's based largely on maturity, which is based largely on their backgrounds.

Maybe I'm wrong, but I've lived long enough and seen enough to believe wholeheartedly that I'm right. I've got the ligament pain and the tomato cravings to prove it.

But if it turns out that I am wrong, I guarantee one thing: there will be a long line of people ready to remind me.

I started taking HGH and I'm TELLING you, I feel like an honest version of Lance Armstrong.

Diamonds Aren't Forever

You want a job with a litany of challenges? You want a job that's filled with unpredictability and guesswork? You want a job where the decisions you make, many of them based on hunches and hope and the forces of an uncontrolled market, might end up costing your team as much as $100 million?

Perfect. Set your sights on becoming a Major League Baseball general manager.

There's no job in sports that's even remotely as difficult.

Name another sport where the performances of star players fluctuate as wildly. Name another sport where a team has to wait as many as five years just to see if a player it drafted in the first round is even good enough to play *at all*. Name another sport where the players are as fragile and the variables are so wild that even a player's age—his *age,* for crying out loud—can't always be taken at face value.

Let's go right to one of the most ridiculous examples: in baseball, there's an actual malady they call Dead Arm Syndrome. It's a real thing. Has its own Wikipedia entry and everything. So if you're the GM, there's a chance the guy you just gave $85 million to $100 million to be your stud for the next five to seven years might walk up to the manager after his first start and say his arm is dead. It happened to the Red Sox and Daisuke Matsuzaka. (Not after his first start, but it happened.) When the Patriots sign Tom Brady to a big extension, they know at least one thing: he's not going to tell Bill Belichick his arm's dead. But you know what happens if he does? The Patriots pay him for the rest of that year and then cut him loose, at no further cost. Our friend the baseball GM doesn't have that option; he's stuck paying out the entire contract—down to the penny—for a dead arm.

When you break it down, it's almost laughable.

It's the closest thing to an impossible job.

Chone Figgins hit .298 and led the league in walks with 101 in 2009 with the Angels. He was good enough to get a few MVP votes. That off-season, he signed a big contract with the Mariners, and about an hour later his career was essentially over. He wasn't particularly old when he signed with Seattle—thirty-two. There were no glaring red flags about his age or his fitness or his desire. He stole forty-two bases his last year with the Angels and forty-two his first year with the Mariners. (That was about the only thing he did well in three years in Seattle.)

What happened? Nobody really knows. He just stopped being a good major-league baseball player, and it cost the Mariners $35 million, including the $8 million they gave him before the 2013 season to simply go away.

In baseball, they shrug and move on.

Oh well. Happens all the time.

It is truly incredible how wildly the performances of baseball players fluctuate when compared with other sports. In basketball, unless there's a serious injury, the decline is gradual. Guys slow down little by little and their playing time decreases along with it. When they announce their retirement, nobody's surprised. Jason Kidd can play for two decades and still be productive providing he's used correctly and he stays healthy.

You can't say the same about a guy like Adrian Beltre. Not to pick on the Mariners again, but when they signed Adrian Beltre from the Dodgers in 2005 they thought they were buying instant contention. In his walk year with the Dodgers, Beltre was a beast: 48 homers, 121 RBIs, a .334 average, OPS of 1.017.

In five years in Seattle, he never even drove in 100 runs. That 1.017 OPS became .716 his first year as a Mariner. He went from Barry Bonds to David Freaking Eckstein over the course of one off-season. And he was *twenty-six* years old! How does that happen? Even factoring in the pitcher-friendly nature of Safeco Field, Beltre's decline was outrageous. The Mariners should have been buying the best years of Beltre's career; instead, about the only things he did consistently in Seattle were play defense and strike out.

Oh, and the Mariners ended up paying Beltre more than $60 million for his efforts. And the next three years of Beltre's career? He drove in at least 100 runs in each of those years and finished third in the American League MVP balloting after a huge year with the Rangers in 2012.

How crazy is that?

You know who took the heat for Beltre's collapse? Well, Beltre took a little of it, but he got to move on and make tons more money and continue an impressive career. The guy who got the bulk of the blame was the general manager, Bill Bavasi, who rode the signings of Figgins and Beltre off into the sunset after the 2008 season. Sure, he looked bad, but how could he have known? It's not like he was the only guy willing to give those two players big, multiyear contracts. He's just the one who got stuck.

It's not just the guys shopping off the rack who get burned. The big-market boys do, too. In his first four years with the Yankees, Mark Teixeira went from being a possible Hall of Fame candidate—his 2009 year was phenomenal—to being an average hitter while playing in a tremendous hitters' park. The deterioration was sudden and inexplicable, but it was real. By the time he was 32, he was just another guy.

The Mets have become a futile franchise. They have attendance problems and identity problems and they've lost the goodwill of most of the fan base. But in 2012, they had one transcendent player: R.A. Dickey.

He wrote a captivating and compelling best seller.

He had a phenomenal season on the mound and won the National League Cy Young Award.

He was a novelty, relying on the knuckleball, a nearly extinct but highly entertaining pitch.

He represented the team well by routinely giving interesting quotes from a generally sour locker room.

He had one bad outing, was a wonderful story, and became one of the few reasons to embrace the franchise.

What happened in the off-season? The Mets traded him to Toronto. They didn't trust his success enough to count on it happening again, and so they took one of their two marketable players (David Wright being the other) and packaged him in a deal that brought a bunch of young prospects.

The trade didn't bring a huge outcry from whatever is left of the Mets' fan base. You know why? They could see the reasoning. Nobody can safely say that R.A. Dickey's 2012 season *wasn't* a fluke. Not even the Blue Jays. Again, there's the difference between the baseball GM and the guys in the other sports: it's rare—*exceedingly* rare—for a football or basketball player in his prime to have one transcendent season and then utterly fail the next season without injury being a factor. In baseball, it happens.

In fact, you can make the case that 40 percent of the time major-league starting pitchers don't have it on the day they start. And that's exactly how they describe it: *I didn't have it today.* And that's acceptable in baseball, because it's just the way things are. A guy making $15 million to make 35 starts sits at his locker and says,

"Well, fellas—just didn't have it today," and everybody nods their heads and moves along. It's nobody's fault.

Imagine being the guy who has to make the case for spending all that money. Your livelihood is linked to so many random, non-scientific factors, and you have no control over any of them.

To cite another example: name the last time an NBA general manager was shocked to learn that his starting center was actually five years older than anybody thought. It happens in baseball often enough for general managers to include it in their research when they're looking to sign a Dominican player.

Let's compare drafts. The NBA draft is two rounds. Every game of every college team is on television or live-streamed over the Internet. The amount of research that is handed to an NBA general manager is astounding.

The baseball draft is a circus. Seriously, I don't know how they can even keep it all straight. They're tossing out names faster than a horse-racing announcer—do we really even know if all these guys really exist? They draft up to forty rounds—plus compensatory picks—and that's an improvement. It used to be that teams could draft until they wanted to stop drafting. If you wanted to stay all night and into the next day picking every one of the owner's nephews and a junior-college pitcher whose dad owns the local Mercedes dealership, knock yourself out. A team could sit all by itself, tossing out names until the GM fell asleep or the phone went dead. Now they say the draft is "up to" forty rounds. You want to pack up after thirty-five rounds because the owner doesn't have any nephews this year, go right ahead. Still, the number of baseball players that must be scouted to fill all the minor-league teams in an organization is astounding.

Say you were an NBA GM at any point between 1993 and 2012 and you had a high draft pick and needed a point guard. I'm not going to say it's been pretty easy to figure it out, but let's just say it hasn't been that hard.

From the '93 draft, when Tim Hardaway was the first point guard taken, to the 2012 draft, when Damian Lillard was the first point guard taken, there have been just two busts among the first point guards taken. Felipe Lopez was a bust, and Mateen Cleaves was a bust. Every other point guard—we're talking only about the first one taken, remember, guys like Allen Iverson and Jason Kidd and even Randy Foye—has been either a solid contributor or a star.

If you fail on back-to-back NBA drafts, you should probably be handcuffed and led out of the team's facility.

Scott Pioli was fired after just four drafts as general manager of the Kansas City Chiefs. Nobody complained about this; most people associated with the team probably thought it was time for Pioli to go. But a quick look at his drafts shows a guy who really didn't do all that poorly when it came to building a team. He drafted Jamaal Charles, Eric Berry, Javier Arenas, Dexter McCluster. He got a Pro Bowl linebacker, Justin Houston, in the third round.

For his first three picks of the 2010 draft, he got Berry, McCluster, and Arenas. Two years later, he was fired.

There was no outrage over his firing. In football, fans have seen Bill Parcells turn a team from 5-11 to 11-5 in one season, largely on the strength of a draft or two. The way it works in the NFL, Pioli had his chance and now it's someone else's turn.

Could you imagine the Cubs firing Theo Epstein—technically not the GM, but he's the guy making the calls—after four years because he didn't turn the Cubs into champions? That's essentially what happened to Pioli, but there would be outrage—crazed outrage—if the Cubs jettisoned Epstein that quickly. Every single baseball writer would attack the Cubs for being callous.

Sorry, but it's just way easier to draft in the other sports, and far harder to screw up. In the NFL, the teams get immediate control of a player after at least three years in college. They have a combine where they can ask anything they damned well please—legitimate or not—and have an English-speaking, college-educated person answer.

Everyone knows the MLB draft is a long-term, hit-or-miss proposition. Draft-eligible baseball players come from high school, junior college, and four-year college. Unless a guy is a college senior, he's got the option to turn down the signing bonus and go back to school, which means general managers have to assess a factor called "signability"—something that doesn't exist in the NBA or NFL. If a GM guesses wrong on signability, as the Pittsburgh Pirates did when they drafted hot-shot Stanford pitcher Mark Appel with the eighth pick of the 2012 draft and he chose to return to school . . . well, the GM looks awfully silly.

And once the players are signed, the fun begins. This is when general managers are handed a whole new set of issues. Even the most elite player is subjected to the minors, which means every player essentially leaves the control of the major-league team and becomes community property within the organization. There are so many steps, so many hands that get ahold of these guys—every change in managers or pitching coaches or hitting coaches could spell disaster. Teams try to monitor these kinds of things, but a bad pitching coach can screw up a prospect for years. A hitting coach who decides to put his stamp on a kid can change the course of a career.

The players drafted in the first round of the MLB draft in 2007 had combined to play one inning in the major leagues by the end of the 2008 season. *One inning!* Sometimes it can take seven years for a top pick to make it to the big leagues. From 18 to 25—you can be a totally different person in seven years.

There are just so many variables for a baseball GM to consider. In the NBA, every hoop is 10 feet off the floor and every court is 94 feet long. In the NFL, every field is 100 yards long and 53 yards wide.

The baseball GM doesn't have the luxury of consistent dimensions. He might have a short right-field fence, which means his scouts have to pay close attention to big left-handed hitters. He might have a pitchers' park or a big outfield or the thin air in Denver, where sinker-ball pitchers are like gold. It's amazing how specific this stuff gets.

Jason Bay can't hit at Citi Field. Well, hell—there goes $66 million.

Mike Hampton can't pitch in Denver. There goes *$121 million!*

In many cases, there's a direct connection between salary and performance. Golf and baseball are the two sports with the most downtime, the most time to think about what you're trying to do and the stakes involved in doing it.

It's exceedingly rare to hear an announcer say, "Oh, Dwyane Wade is really pressing out there." Sometimes you'll see an NBA player or an NFL quarterback try to do too much, but in baseball it's an entirely different animal.

Big contracts screw up some players. Barry Zito was affected by the money when he got his huge deal in San Francisco. Albert Pujols couldn't hit for the first month of his first season with the Angels.

It's like Greg Norman: fantastic on Saturday, ghastly on Sunday. Why? The money's out there, and psychology gets involved.

Has there ever been a player comparable to Alex Rodriguez in another sport who so obviously and repeatedly gagged when the lights got brightest? Remember the divisional series against the Tigers in 2006, when Joe Torre had to drop him to the eighth spot in the lineup? One of the best hitters in baseball was reduced to being a Double-A hitter. He was completely overmatched, and it was all in his head.

The adverse psychological effects of outside influences— money, attention—are profoundly exaggerated in baseball. How does a GM account for that?

How does he account for chemistry? The season is so long and the travel is so ridiculous that you have to take into account how personalities will work together. You get Milton Bradley in the clubhouse and he can blow it up. You might as well just pack it in.

There's just so much, and that's without even mentioning the lack of a salary cap—"Mo' money, mo' problems," says Biggie Smalls—or the battle for regional television deals or the fifteen- to twenty-year PED train that drove right through the center of the sport.

A great job? Oh, yeah, sure it is. It's so great, everyone who gets one of them should demand two perks: a lifetime supply of Advil and Pepcid AC.

The Big Ten is changing division names from Leaders and Legends to "Will Lose Annually to Urban Meyer" and "Will Lose But Less Regularly."

When Small Grows Up

American sports culture is dominated by team sports, and the broadcasting world follows that lead. Most of our reporting is on teams, and most of the fan interest revolves around teams and not individuals. Guys wear jerseys of players on their favorite teams; rarely, if ever, do you see a guy dressing up like Rafael Nadal to head out to a tennis match. That guy's not a fan; he's a stalker.

There used to be a time when quirky, nonteam, nonmainstream sports found a sizable audience. The flagship show was called *Wide World of Sports,* and you could find everything from barrel jumping to cliff diving. Comedian Norm McDonald once cracked, "There's only two types of cliff divers: successful ones, and stuff on a rock."

That's how most NFL fans probably feel as they watch their team try to find its next franchise quarterback through the draft. You either hit the lottery with Aaron Rodgers (our figurative successful cliff diver) or you spend several years trying to convince yourself that David Carr (our figurative . . . well, you know) will eventually flourish.

You wouldn't think it would be that difficult. You'd think great quarterbacking would follow a linear progression. The best high school quarterbacks go to the top college powerhouses and usually get the benefit of the best coaching. By this logic, it figures that simply drafting the star signal-caller from your top fifteen to twenty collegiate juggernauts would result in a predictable line of success.

And yet it's anything but predictable. In 2013, there are as many starting NFL quarterbacks (one) from Eastern Illinois,

Utah, Nevada, Delaware, and Miami of Ohio as there are from Oklahoma, Michigan, USC, and Virginia Tech. There are two from North Carolina State (Philip Rivers and—for most of his career—Russell Wilson) but none from Alabama, Boise State, Oregon, Florida, Texas, or Nebraska.

This is one of those quirks in sports—and life—that make no sense. On first glance, it seems outrageous that so many quarterbacks who were ignored by big-time college programs have gone on to become not only NFL starters but Pro Bowl players and Super Bowl winners.

Let's take a look at the top fifteen college-football programs in America over the past five years (2008–13) based on an admittedly subjective criteria of wins, big wins, national profile, momentum, and stability. In alphabetical order: Alabama, Boise State, Florida, Georgia, LSU, Nebraska, Ohio State, Oklahoma, Oregon, Stanford, Texas, USC, Virginia Tech, West Virginia, and Wisconsin.

In a league of thirty-two teams, there are only six quarterbacks from those fifteen schools. Several of them, including the Jets' Mark Sanchez, the Cardinals' Carson Palmer, and the Eagles' Michael Vick, appear to be on the verge of breathing their last NFL breath.

This isn't a recent trend. Dan Fouts, Terry Bradshaw, Brett Favre—all products of lower-tier programs, all Hall of Famers. Brady Quinn, Matt Leinart, Colt McCoy—all products of marquee programs, all journeymen.

For a three-year period, Kurt Warner was the best quarterback in the NFL. He went to the University of Northern Iowa, played in the Arena League, and bagged groceries. During the late 1990s and early 2000s, he was better than any quarterback produced by Florida State, Alabama, or USC.

Seems almost impossible, doesn't it? However, if you dig a

little bit and explore some of the underlying reasons, it makes perfect sense.

I can relate it to a study on human physiology released in the fall of 2012 by the University of Copenhagen. The study showed that people who exercised for thirty minutes a day lost more weight and were healthier than people who exercised sixty minutes a day. Wait . . . how could that be? Obviously, more exercise is better—burns more calories, increases cardiovascular strength, tones the body. It seems utterly counterintuitive to believe that less exercise can produce more results.

But, looking deeper, you see the researchers' findings were backed by common sense. Guys who worked out for sixty minutes didn't do anything the rest of the day; those who worked out for thirty were less tired and, therefore, more active. Exercising for sixty minutes increases hunger, and many of those study members ate their way past their workout.

Work out less, lose more weight. It would seem to make absolutely no sense, and yet it's absolutely true.

Along those same lines, it makes absolutely no sense that BYU, with Jim McMahon and Steve Young, has produced two Super Bowl–winning quarterbacks, the exact same number as Notre Dame.

Makes no sense.

And yet absolutely true.

Just like the exercise study, the small-school quarterback phenomenon makes more and more sense the deeper you dive into it.

Here's one obvious and slightly pedestrian reason: in high school and college, practice and workout times are limited because of NCAA rules or the practicalities of schoolwork. This puts a disproportionate emphasis on talent at those levels. But once a quarterback arrives in the NFL, he can work as long and hard as he wishes. He can sleep in the film room and be in the weight room at 5 a.m. As NFL schemes—both offense and defense—grow more complex, a quarterback's talent becomes less important as his work ethic, study habits, and intellectual dexterity become more crucial. Workaholics tend to do better. An elite talent with a questionable work ethic (JaMarcus Russell and Ryan Leaf, to name two famous examples) can spell disaster or just underachievement (Jeff George and Michael Vick).

JaMarcus Russell was the ideal college quarterback. He was 6 feet 6 inches, 270 pounds; moved like a running back; and could throw the ball 70 yards from one knee. Playing with all the speedy receivers at LSU, he looked like a guy who could be great for a decade. I was doing the NFL Draft for ESPN when he was picked No. 1 by the Raiders in 2007, and when I shook his hand I was amazed at how big it was. It seems crazy, and it blew me away at the time, but Russell was bigger than Gaines Adams, a *defensive end* from Clemson who was drafted three picks later. Russell failed, though—he failed in that part of the game that requires a guy to spend sixty hours a week learning his craft. He failed in the film room.

The second factor became apparent to me when I was spending time in the locker room covering Trent Dilfer. He was a quarterback of his time: a guy who wasn't particularly fast, didn't leave the pocket unless it was necessary, and had a reputation for being able to stand strong against a pass rush. Even though he didn't move much and wasn't susceptible to open-field hits, his body was a mess after games. If you looked at his arms, neck, and chest, you would have been convinced he got into a fight with either a barbed-wire fence or a cat on meth.

I've interviewed plenty of college quarterbacks after games, too, and I've never noticed the same physical toll. In the NFL, a quarterback faces three hours of contact from bigger and stronger athletes. It's an integral part of the job. From the first exhibition game forward, he's playing with some degree of injury. His ability to deal with those physical challenges goes a long way toward determining his success.

When Dilfer came to work at ESPN years later, he confirmed my observations. He told me toughness is the most underrated part of being an NFL quarterback. That led me to the following theory: many of the big-school stars aren't prepared for the next level because they haven't been subjected to the same physical test. In relative terms, they've been coddled.

At the premier programs, a quarterback spends three or four years surrounded by the best high school offensive linemen, backs, tight ends, and receivers. He is sacked infrequently—in fact, he's rarely even put in an uncomfortable position. He has a strong running game, so defenses don't often have the luxury of a balls-out pass rush. His receivers create separation against inferior defenders, and his pass protection is unlike anything he'll ever experience in the NFL.

Let me ask you this: Didn't Matt Barkley, at USC, have better wide receivers than the Browns, Jets, and Bills have right now?

Big-school quarterbacks are like trust-fund kids. When they jump from their college programs to the NFL, it's like going from a life sailing on the Cape to a sixty-hour-a-week job. A lot of them can't handle it, and NFL teams see that right away. They don't have any patience with that, so you see guys like Matt Leinart bounce around and never reach their potential.

Conversely, at the smaller and less-heralded schools, the quarterback plays with mediocre talent. He doesn't have anything close to the same pass protection or running game or receivers. He's already accustomed to delivering the football through tighter windows. Improvisation—out of necessity—has been woven into his DNA. This creates a toughness and resilience that is paramount to success at the NFL level.

There's a psychological aspect to this, as well. The guy who's been overlooked throughout the process, from the college-recruiting side to the NFL draft side, is pissed off. He sees the guys who were recruited to the bigger and better programs. He sees the guys who were drafted ahead of him. He's got something to prove. The chip on his shoulder is big, and he can use it to his benefit.

Tom Brady started at Michigan, but he was constantly fighting off Drew Henson and the hype that surrounded him. His draft snub—taken in the sixth round—resulted in him playing with a level of anger that remains inside him to this day. Even the NFL's most talented and highest-paid quarterback, Aaron Rodgers, was forced to go the junior-college route because he was a late-bloomer who grew up in a place (Chico, California) scouts rarely visited. He ended up at Cal only after Jeff Tedford came to one of his junior-college games to scout a tight end. The competitiveness you see in Rodgers is the product of all of that. (After everything he's accomplished, teammates say he still gets testy when teased about his height.)

What are NFL teams seeking when they scout a quarterback? Guys who can make plays. That's exactly the quality sought by second-tier college programs. Jim McIlwaine was the offensive coordinator at Alabama before becoming head coach at Colorado State. He told me his hopes for the quarterback were modest: don't lose the game; let the defense win it.

Could you imagine Baylor's defensive coordinator telling Robert Griffin III the same thing before a game with Texas? It would be outrageous to even consider. Yet at the top programs, ball control and game management are often primary concerns.

Greg Cosell has been watching tons of film for years as a producer for NFL Films. He says one of the best attributes a quarterback can have is the ability to throw in a muddied pocket. If a guy can sidestep a defensive end and pump-fake a nose tackle and still keep his eyes downfield, that guy has a chance to make it in the NFL.

Think about how many times Roethlisberger is praised for his ability to improvise inside the pocket, to avoid the rush and free himself just long enough to get off a pass. Where do you think he learned that? Not in the NFL, that's for sure. He learned that playing at Miami of Ohio, behind an offensive line that didn't have any five-star recruits.

Matt Ryan saw a lot of muddy pockets at Boston College. So did Flacco, at Delaware. So did Eli Manning, at Ole Miss. They were constantly under duress, being pushed one direction or the other, forced to go through their progressions as they dealt with chaos in front of them.

The only times Barkley and Leinart saw muddy pockets at USC was when they were watching Ryan or Roethlisberger or Manning on television. They weren't watching Flacco; his team wasn't on TV.

This trend doesn't figure to end anytime soon. At least not before 2014, because most NFL draft gurus predict Louisville's Teddy Bridgewater—the best football player at a basketball school—will be the first quarterback taken in the 2014 draft.

Nobody believes the path to future NFL stardom should begin in the Mid American Conference. The big programs are still going to get the highest-rated high school quarterbacks and surround them with the highest-rated offensive linemen, wide receivers, and running backs.

But the evidence *does* suggest something fascinating: the guys who dominate our television screens on Saturdays aren't the ones who will dominate them on Sundays.

Same guy and same car parked at a strip club at 10 a.m. and 10 p.m. Why does he feel so much more pathetic parked there earlier? Never underestimate the importance of the time you do something.

I Value What I Need

First, an experiment. Please indulge me for a moment; it won't take up much time, and you'll see the results rather quickly.

The next time your wife asks you to run a few errands, I want you to change it up a little. Ad lib, improvise, think outside the box. Consider it your version of a double reverse on third and inches.

When you're asked to pick up milk, eggs, and bread, stop by Home Depot instead and grab a garden hose. Buy a rake on your way out even though you've got a good one at home and no use for an extra one. Stop at the grocery store and grab some olives and licorice. The idea is to seek value over need.

Obviously, this could create some tension at home. She's going to wonder what you were thinking and how she's going to make dinner with a rake and a garden hose.

"Wait a minute," you will say in your best lecturing tone, *"let me explain how much value you got in return."*

Tell her you found a coupon for the garden hose, the olives were buy one get one free, and the licorice was 60 percent off. And the rake? Oh, the rake.

"Honey, they were practically giving that thing away."

How does this pertain to sports? Easy: it's the exact same brand of nonsense NFL teams shovel down the media's throats after every draft.

Value is a word that's easy to sell. Everyone supports value. How couldn't you? But I have a different question: Can value actually cost a team wins and money?

Your team's secondary regularly gets torched, but instead of drafting the best available cornerback, it decides to grab a backup quarterback instead. Why? Because he was a "value pick." In other words, he was just too talented to pass up even though the team already has a star quarterback.

The New York Giants have Eli Manning, a two-time Super Bowl champion quarterback. He hasn't missed a start in eight years and probably has another six years left in his arm. You could argue that Manning is just hitting his prime. And yet, on draft day 2013, the Giants drafted Syracuse quarterback Ryan Nassib—all in the name of value. The Giants had real needs to address, but they fell into the value trap.

Hey, Giants fans . . . hope you like the rake. You're out of milk and your kids want cereal, but now you have two rakes to take care of business when the autumn leaves begin to fall.

I know what you're thinking:

Colin, who are you to tell Giants GM Jerry Reese what to do?

It's an age-old argument: you aren't allowed to criticize someone for doing his job unless you've not only done the same job but done it better. That's ridiculous, and in this case it ignores some important facts.

1. Judging football talent is not rocket science.
2. Judging football talent is not an exact science.

Even highly regarded football executives make mistakes—big, steaming mistakes—and they make them more often than you might imagine. Take a look at the Denver Broncos. They're rightfully given credit for signing Peyton Manning, but they've whiffed on two high-profile draft picks in the past decade. Their choice of Tim Tebow in the first round in 2010 and their 2005 fifth-round pick of Maurice Clarett were both widely mocked by fans and the media as soon as they were announced. This wasn't a case of hindsight.

Guess what?

In both cases, the fans and media were right.

We know all about Tebow's shortcomings, so no need to rehash that topic. But Clarett ran a 4.8 forty-yard dash at the scouting combine—only slightly faster than a grocery cart and far slower than the average for a tailback. He was so bad Mike Shanahan made him essentially the first cut of training camp. Everyone saw this coming—everyone, it seems, except Bronco executives.

A "lay" person debating NFL picks—whether the layperson is a radio host or a construction worker—is not the same as a dentist arguing with an antitrust attorney over state and federal trade practices. The attorney, with an advanced degree in antitrust law, is an expert and the dentist is not. Debating NFL picks is not the same as a car salesman arguing with a cardiothoracic surgeon over a heart-valve replacement.

The surgeon is an expert.

The car salesman is not.

Even top NFL executives rely heavily on regional scouts whose level of acumen ranges from genius to barely employed. Those scouts file hundreds of reports on players in their area. Poor evaluations happen.

The vagaries of the profession lead us to one point: value is staggeringly overrated unless accompanied by need. This isn't exclusive to the NFL; it applies to almost any business.

Think of an NFL roster as a grocery store.

Shelf space is limited.

Some items are perishable.

Budgets are a necessary evil.

If NFL teams were pawnshops, the calculus would be different. Watches, old maps, and baseball cards, over time, can grow in value. Milk and bread don't. Expensive items sitting on the shelf—or, in our case, the bench—are nothing more than wasted revenue.

Nobody would argue that acquiring players at the right price is a crucial aspect of building a team. Overpaying for a tight end might manifest itself in an inability to land a defensive tackle you desperately need. But what's the point of passing on a player who plays a position of need in favor of a player you know will sit for several years or never play?

The two deepest rosters in the current NFL are in Seattle and San Francisco. Both the Seahawks and the 49ers have used the past two drafts to "reach" for players because they had a need at a particular position—value be damned.

Lacking playmakers on offense, the 49ers took Oregon running back LaMichael James in 2012. The Seahawks chose pass-rushing specialist Bruce Irvin in the first round, as many as two rounds higher than most teams felt he should be picked. In the 2013 draft, the 49ers traded up to grab safety Eric Reid from LSU; again, the pick was higher than most had predicted Reid to go, but it was meant to fill a need. Both clubs are bucking the concept of "value" drafting, and both are at the top of the league.

Many don't see the value—pun intended—in drafting for need.

New England coach Bill Belichick has a fantastic resume, but he has been inconsistent with draft picks. He chose Arkansas quarterback Ryan Mallett in the third round of the 2011 draft even though the Pats' defense was—and is—ranked near the bottom of the NFL. Mallett was chosen as a value pick even though Tom Brady had said a year earlier that he planned on playing another ten years.

You don't have to be a genius or a second-guesser to find several players who would have been more valuable to the Pats than

Mallett. In fact, let's take two examples from the same team: Pro Bowl cornerback Richard Sherman and top rookie linebacker K.J. Wright were chosen after Mallet by the Seahawks. No fewer than twenty-six cornerbacks were taken after Mallett, and many— Sherman, Chris Culliver of the 49ers, Chykie Brown of the Ravens—would start for a New England team so weak at the position that they've resorted to using receivers.

Mallett, the value pick, has yet to take a meaningful snap in the league.

His value is difficult to assess from the bench.

There's always a counterpoint, right? Sports and politics were invented to fuel the art of the endless argument. And if you're going to counter my need-over-value argument, you're probably going to start with one name: Aaron Rodgers. The Packers chose Rodgers in the first round even though Brett Favre was still slingin' and winnin' at Lambeau Field. Rodgers sat for two years while a good Packers team could have used a player from that position of that draft in other areas.

But look closer: Favre was in his fifteenth year in the league, and the retirement talk had already started. Ted Thompson, a new general manager, wanted to find a successor to Favre and simultaneously put his own stamp on the franchise. Favre was notoriously stubborn and unwilling to adapt for the betterment of the franchise. Rodgers, an elite talent who was under consideration to be the No. 1 overall pick, was the logical choice to draft and sit for two years. The same arguments can't be made for Mallett or Nassib.

A lot of old-line baseball people scoffed at the evidence-based analytics employed by Oakland Athletics general manager Billy Beane. Those advanced statistics, used to unearth undervalued skills and documented by author Michael Lewis in *Moneyball,* are now used in some form or another by every team in Major League Baseball.

By their very nature, sports are about rules, both official and unofficial. Once we latch on to them, we tend to hold on with a death grip. We cherish the histories of our sports and guard them like a junkyard Rottweiler. What has worked in the past should work in the future and all that. But the people who run sports teams are becoming more open and less tethered to tradition. Many come from Ivy League backgrounds and are paid to inject new ideas into old institutions. Hunches and gut feelings are—thankfully—being replaced by intelligence and reasoning.

The NFL, despite its modern trappings, is the last sport to adopt quantitative analysis. Slowly, though, you can see the cavalry kicking up dust on the trail. The revolution is coming, and someday we'll look back and realize value without need serves no purpose.

Your NFL team needs the staples: milk, eggs, and bread. Don't let them try to convince you that licorice, even at 60 percent off, is a legitimate substitute.

There're several different life insurance policies most of us could buy, but they all give me the creeps. There's whole life, term life, and variable life, just to name a few.

If I inadvertently get crushed by a bread truck—and who really wants to, so it's almost always an accident—my wife will get a nice payout from Disney. They own ESPN. I could probably afford to buy a more lucrative policy but frankly, who wants to give her any crazy ideas? Secondly, and perhaps this is selfish—OK, it absolutely is—why would I want her to live a better life once I'm buried next to insects? There's no need for a second Kardashian family.

Oh please, like she wants me vacationing in the Hamptons or driving in a convertible down the Pacific Coast Highway with a bombshell once she dies. She should have enough for food, clothing, and the occasional night out, you know, at a local gas station.

The entire life insurance industry is based on payouts after life. Some investment.

So instead I purchase Sports Life Insurance. It's foolproof and nobody has to kick the bucket for a payout. In fact, it delivers in some way almost every time. Think about that—straight cash without the embalming fluid.

Sports Life Insurance is simply betting against your favorite teams.

Years ago in Las Vegas while I was transferring from fandom to broadcasting, it really hit me. Every time one of my favorite football teams lost, it ruined my weekend. Especially college football, where one loss can discombobulate a season. Since most men get grumpier as they age (a British study says men over 50 laugh as rarely as two and a half times a day), who wouldn't want to avoid surly weekends?

So I began betting against all my teams and the result is obvious. If my team wins, I party like a rock star, or at least one that goes to bed by 9:45 p.m. If my team gets shelled, well, I still partially win.

Now the only drawback, of course, is that you are always, at least partially, a loser. A slight kick to the shin. There is never pure nirvana, yet you never spend a weekend with the shades drawn and sharp knives scattered about, either. In betting parlance, the partial win covers the spread—and the pain.

Listen, if you want to spend your life taking wild emotional turns, count me out. You try to turn two bases into a triple, I'll just stand here at second base, admiring my commendable work. Hey, nobody ever got fired after leading the league in doubles.

For those interested, this policy is available online and in a certain city with lots of neon. There is no money-back guarantee, just money back, guaranteeing certain football weekends are slightly brighter.

Don't allow someone with no life to ruin yours.

The Drain Game

As a kid, I hated math but loved sports. It never seemed like a conflict. They were mutually exclusive, right? Only later did I come to an important realization: sports is largely nothing *but* numbers. You can't be an educated sports fan without some level of mathematical literacy. It's just not possible.

Derek Jeter wears No. 2, MJ wore 23, and Magic wore 32. Seven-hundred fifty-five is Hank Aaron's home-run total. There are sixty-eight teams in March Madness; the scholarship limit in college football is 85. If I say 100 points, you instinctively say Wilt. You don't have to be a Yankee fan to know that fifty-six straight games with a hit means Joe DiMaggio. Bill Russell has 11 NBA titles as a Celtic player; Phil Jackson has the same as an NBA head coach.

Every sports fan has a little Russell Crowe *Beautiful Mind* thing working when it comes to sports. We argue and bet on the numbers. You rank players and teams, elevating and degrading, based on those same numbers.

There are two lesser-known numbers that might be the most staggering and important in professional sports: 60 and 78.

According to a story in *Sports Illustrated* by Pablo S. Torre, 60 percent of NBA players are broke within five years of retirement. It seems impossible, but football players are worse: the study showed 78 percent of NFL players went bankrupt after two years of retirement.

It's nothing short of unbelievable, but the numbers—it's always the numbers—back it up.

Fans have a hard time coming to terms with such a wild paradox. How can people who have so much end up with so little?

Whenever I've watched MTV's *Cribs* or any other show glori-
fying the wealth of professional athletes, I come away with an odd
mix of pity and bewilderment. On one hand, I completely understand: after a childhood of struggle and hardship—as is the case
with many athletes—who wouldn't display some extravagance? It's
natural to want to surround yourself with outward symbols of your
hard work and status.

Those television shows that give a voyeur's-eye look into the
mansions of hip-hop moguls and star athletes could just as easily be
renamed *My Garage Is Bigger Than Anything You'll Ever Own*.
From gold-plated bathtubs to diamond-encrusted cutting boards,
it's a step-by-step guide to the excess of the celebrity lifestyle.

I don't admire the 15,000-square-foot castles. I don't resent
them, either.

At the Union Plaza in Las Vegas, I once met a tanned, tall
Texan in his early sixties. Drinking whiskey on the rocks and drawl-
ing out story after story, he told me he had recently sold several
television stations in his home state. He came from a large family
and possessed the confidence and perspective of a man who had
been successful but had to fight for it.

In the middle of one of his stories, he looked up from his
glass and said, "If you resent success, you will never achieve it. Be
excited about it, even if the success is not your own. Bitter people
are rarely happy or successful." Everything he said after that might
as well have been an inaudible hum. Twenty years later that sentiment still resonates with me: celebrate the success of others.

That's why it nags at me when I become vaguely depressed
watching young athletes parading around their paradise pointing
out all the sunken, pool-sized bathtubs and lavish theater rooms. I
want to celebrate their successes, and I do, but it's hard when you
can visualize the repo man, a few years into the future, knocking

on the back door. It's hard to be in a celebratory mood when you see your favorite NFL tight end squander $3.6 million on his retro jersey collection, only to have the IRS confiscate it for unpaid taxes.

Let me repeat: I don't resent the money. I am astonished, however, when I see what all that money becomes.

The question that needs to be asked—how in the hell can you blow through so much money so fast?—is only partially answered by the images in those shows.

It almost seems like it just disappears. *Poof,* like a magic trick. Scottie Pippen made $120 million, according to estimates, and has since fallen into financial ruin. Did he shower in Cristal for a decade? Is his roof made of diamonds? Former NBA player Antoine Walker lost $110 million and can't blame a penny of it on Bernie Madoff. Do these guys have single-use, disposable Armani suits?

Well, the complete explanation might not be as easy as it seems. There are several factors at work, and just one of them is ridiculous spending.

Robert Raiola is a certified public accountant who specializes in sports and entertainment and calls himself Sports Tax Man. According to him, the first order of business for the disbelieving fans is to understand that athletes don't actually get all the money you read about.

Of course, we all understand taxes and most of us understand that athletes must pay agents and business managers, but sometimes those facts get lost in the haze of the headlines. When you see a story about a Los Angeles Dodger signing a contract for $96 million over four years, an easy vision springs to mind: $24 million a year.

However, Raiola will tell you that our $96 million Dodger is taking home $11 million a year. Before you start playing an imaginary violin, let me be clear: I'm not asking you to cry for a guy who brings home eight figures a year.

But . . . but.

The public, including the player's family and friends and associates and interior decorators and other assorted hangers-on, sees one thing: the headline. The $24 million a year. And what's a million here or there when you're pocketing 24?

Let's break it down:

Gross wages:	$24,642,857
Agent's fees (5 percent):	$1,232,143
Net wages:	$23,410,714
Federal income tax:	$8,426,902
CA income tax:	$3,222,041
Social Security:	$7,049
Medicare:	$357,321
Medicare surtax:	$219,536
Tax subtotal:	$12,232,849
NET CASH:	$11,177, 865

Granted, that's still a lot of lettuce, but it's not $24 million worth. It doesn't stop there; California has higher real-estate costs, higher food costs, higher gas costs. And all of that points to the root of a bigger problem with young multimillionaire athletes: financial illiteracy.

The ESPN "30 for 30" documentary *Broke* did an outstanding job of bringing the depth of the problem to life. These guys who earn huge salaries rarely have the perspective those stark numbers above bring. They don't think about the short duration of their careers or the beauty of saving a ton of that money in order to make the rest of their lives that much more comfortable. They feel they can buy their mom and dad a big house and a couple of nice cars. They can take care of their brothers and sisters and nieces and nephews and whoever else comes crawling back into their lives to get a piece of the action. They don't see that water on a rock—drip, drip, drip—eventually creates a big hole. When you're 25 and loaded, perspective is for other people. It's not your world.

Many of these players come from nothing, and going from nothing to everything is overwhelming. They go from a world with nothing but limits to one that's limitless. They might have spent three or four years in college, but they're ignorant of the most basic financial acumen.

After *Broke,* I called former New England Patriot and New York Jet Damien Woody, now one of ESPN's sharpest analysts. He told me, "My tenth or eleventh year in the league, I would start talking to younger guys, just telling them basic stuff. Open up a checking account. Many didn't even understand how to do that. That is scary. Guys get millions and don't even understand how to balance a checkbook."

Open up a checking account. Is there a more telling indictment of the system than those five words? Woody's not exaggerating, either. On the HBO series *Hard Knocks,* the cameras went inside the Cincinnati Bengals' training camp for a rare look at the inner workings and relationships in the game we love. Chad Ochocinco, at the time an established, well-paid star receiver, needed to have head coach Marvin Lewis explain to him how a bank works.

"They come into the league entitled," Woody said. "I came in the league in awe; many guys now think, 'I'm supposed to be here.' They think, 'I'm rich and invincible.' I would tell 'em, 'You're living in fantasy land now, you're still a young man when you leave this game.'

"I probably get about four or five guys a year who call me with money trouble. Looking for something. I just tell 'em, 'I would rather help you instead of giving you cash I'll never get back. Let's solve the problem.'"

Extravagant spending combined with a lack of fiscal acumen is a vicious recipe. Since the latter will never be fully mastered, especially for 21-year-old athletes who never had much and are understandably near-sighted, maybe it's time for jocks to look deep within themselves and ask the really tough questions.

Do I really need a second purple speedboat named after my aunt?
Does my backyard need its own zip code?
Nine bathrooms? Could I possibly make do with six?
Did I really need that helipad on the roof of the vacation home?

Those questions are the small questions that lead to the big, deeper, more personal questions: When are you going to grow up and be accountable? When are you going to judge your worth on something more than what you own?

Maybe, instead of room-sized tanks filled with exotic fish, more athletes should invest in television stations in Texas.

It gets back to the numbers: 60 percent of NBA players, 78 percent of NFL players. And the horrible truth is, it could be worse. Occasionally you'll hear the ugly story of a crooked agent stealing money, but the vast majority of athletes use league-certified agents and money managers who watch over their athletes and try to warn them when the spending gets out of hand. And yes, you're reading that correctly: the agents are the good guys. Where would the bankruptcy numbers be without them?

Honestly, though, with or without agents, how can we expect

young star athletes to understand finances when nobody in their family or social circle has ever dealt with extreme wealth? Would I have a deep and abiding understanding of dentistry or taxidermy at 22 years old unless someone close to me dealt with cavities or the carcasses of dead animals?

Sports is a uniquely kind and cruel business. There may be no clearer example of the extremes of capitalism. The bankruptcy stories are cautionary tales of ambition and riches without the knowledge or discipline to maintain either. It's a single-car crash at the intersection of I'm on Top of the World and I Can No Longer Afford That Bentley.

The average American millionaire is 57 years old, has attended college, and is married. The average NBA rookie earns his first millions at 21. He's single with one year of college and little or no business background. The 57-year-old has earned money for a long time and—with some savvy investing and continued hard work—can continue to earn for years. The average NBA rookie, on average, will be out of the league in six years. With those numbers as a backdrop, can anybody be truly surprised so many athletes end up broke once the revenue stream dries up?

Do you want to know what happens to the money, the fortunes, the castles, and the SUV collections? It all gets lost in a sad fog of ignorance and naiveté and invincibility and near-sightedness. Once you hear the stories and look at the numbers and understand the culture, it's almost predictable.

Nine bathrooms, ten cars, three houses, and zero financial intelligence—in the end, like so much of sports, it all goes back to the math.

If Dallas Cowboy fans want to know why they haven't been in a Super Bowl in twenty years, this may address the issue: they struggle with even the easy stuff. The kind of thing the Steelers, Patriots, Packers, or New York Giants handle in-house becomes a public circus with the Cowboys.

This story sums up the franchise:

Bill Callahan is their offensive coordinator and offensive line coach. He announced he will be calling plays this season. Then when someone asked head coach Jason Garrett about that . . . he clammed up. No comment. Anyone think he could be a little sensitive since he's been calling plays in previous seasons?

This is so typical of the Cowboys. Jerry Jones goes out the day before and sets the fire. He tells reporters the team has a new play-caller, but they have to figure out who it is by watching practice. Callahan announces it's him, but Garrett won't confirm it and even Jerry—when pressed, just to tease the reporters—says he won't disclose it, either. Then why bring it up?

Grocery stores have very thin margins, maybe 3 or 4 percent. What does that mean? Every penny counts. It's similar in the NFL.

Everything and everybody is built to be 8-8. The best teams draft last; there are salary caps and shared revenue streams. So the difference is slight between good to average to bad.

Therefore, details matter—except in Dallas. There's a reason you've had two of the worst drafts in league history over the last twelve years.

The Cowboys are the show *Hard Knocks* without the HBO part. In Dallas, they just call it . . . Monday.

Pack your own lunch in life. Mom isn't around to make it anymore.

Whistle-Blower

Curt Schilling kept a book on umpires. During guest appearances on my show after his career ended, he provided details on how closely he watched umpires to find tendencies that might give him even the smallest edge. He knew that a particular umpire's habit of adding a couple of inches to the plate with two strikes could be the difference between escaping a rough seventh inning or getting yanked. He pitched to these tendencies.

I found this fascinating on a number of levels. Schilling had no problem telling the world about his scrutiny of umpires. He carried the book around with him and kept it in his locker. He updated it constantly. It became part of Schilling Lore, one of the many aspects of his obsessive preparation. He told me matter-of-factly that this was an understood, totally acceptable part of his game.

The idea that someone might question this probably comes as a surprise.

I asked Schilling: Why is this acceptable? Well, as Schilling said . . . it just is. Why wouldn't it be? Referees and officials are human. They are part of the game—often a *big* part. Closely monitored, they can be linked to predictable results that can be used for the player's benefit. The smart player—pitcher, hitter, offensive tackle—takes advantage of everything he can.

But let me ask you this: Can you imagine the media uproar and widespread cynicism that would greet an NBA player who carried around a book that documented the tendencies of referees?

Imagine this scene: Dwyane Wade, before a playoff game, sitting at his locker with a pen and a notebook, writing, "We have Ed Malloy tonight, and I keep a book on Ed. He has certain tendencies I'm confident I can manipulate to help us win."

How would that go over?

Oh.

My.

God.

Could you imagine?

Within seconds of those words hitting the airwaves, Wade and the league would be backpedaling faster than the best NFL cornerback.

Why would it be different? Isn't the hypothetical Wade comment exactly the same as what Schilling told me?

Schilling, smart player.

Wade, smart player.

What's the big deal?

Simple: the NBA, more than any other sports organization in history, has had the integrity of its officiating questioned.

It's the same, but it's not the same.

When the NBA promoted David Stern from executive vice president to commissioner in 1984, it was a dreary league with lots of empty arenas and dwindling star power. Stern energized the NBA by marketing its top stars to a degree never before seen in an American sports league. This marketing push increased ratings and revenue, but it had the unintended consequence of increasing suspicion that the NBA gave its stars—those guys leading the marketing campaign—preferential treatment.

True or not, this ignores a built-in fact about the sport: basketball, at any level, is the one team sport where outcomes can be determined by one incredibly talented performer.

A dominating pitcher has limitations. He needs defense and run support.

A dominating quarterback has limitations. He needs a good offensive line and a stout defense. (After winning the Super Bowl following the 2010 season, Aaron Rodgers went two years with just one playoff win because of a poor line and shaky defense.)

But in the NBA, the Cleveland Cavaliers were the worst team in the league before they landed LeBron James with first pick in the 2003 NBA draft. With very little—other than role players—to surround him, the Cavs became one of the NBA's elite clubs in short order.

This is why critics of the league and its officiating fail to see a broader point.

Superstars in the NBA virtually ensure playoff appearances. The lack of one hugely inhibits your future.

It has nothing to do with the guys blowing the whistles. Nothing at all.

Of course, the conspiracy theorists have their own side to tell. Much of the time it starts with Tim Donaghy, the former referee now banned for life for tampering with the outcomes of games. (For the record, Donaghy claims only to have officiated with an eye on point spreads and not who won or lost.)

Donaghy came on my radio show in March of 2013, just before the release of his book, *Personal Foul.* It was a spirited debate, and Donaghy made several claims that figure to provide more fodder for the conspiracy folks:

The league is still tampering with games.

The refs have agendas.

The league helps the Lakers win.

The league dictates the stars get favorable treatment.

I have no doubt Donaghy believes what he says, but he's guilty of misinterpretation. And because of his reputation and history, the people who want to believe the worst will cling to Donaghy's words, even if they're coming from a guy whose atrocious judgment cost him his marriage, his career, his reputation, and the two years of his life that he spent in a federal prison.

Let's break down one of his claims: long-time ref Dick Bavetta "always said it's good for the Lakers to win, and there's numerous games documented where he was an official for a [Lakers] elimination game . . . and the Lakers always seemed to win."

So let me see if I've got this right: Bavetta says it's good for the Lakers to win.

That's controversial?

Really—*that's* all you've got?

Let's see. By most objective measures, it's good for college basketball if Duke wins, good for college football if Notre Dame wins, good for baseball if the Yankees win.

But somehow thinking it's good for the NBA if the Lakers win is a revelation worthy of Watergate-level outrage?

When traditional powers advance in every sport, it's good for television ratings, which makes it good for the bottom line, which makes it good for every employee of the league. This isn't news, even if it is a sentiment uttered by one official to another in a locker room or lounge after a game.

After a decade in sports radio, I can confidently say I have a little credibility on at least one issue: the hubris, tough talk, and chest thumping of men involved in sports. Every e-mail and tweet is full of all those qualities—it's like a rite of passage for the American male.

Donaghy also sidesteps something that might be worth mentioning: over the past forty years, the Lakers have advanced in many playoff series.

Why?

Because the Lakers have been really, really good for a really, really long time.

It's one of the most glamorous and well-run franchises in North American sports history. If you were to name the all-time Laker starting five, you'd probably leave out Wilt Chamberlain and Shaquille O'Neal—two of the best six centers *in the history of the game*. The guy you'd pick, Kareem Abdul-Jabbar, just happens to be the leading scorer *in the history of the game*.

It is okay if we inject some common sense into the discussion, isn't it?

Good. Just checking.

The Lakers win because they routinely have the kind of talent every other team would die to have.

Another Donaghy blockbuster: the league office would send out tapes to officials, giving them tips to signal specific infractions to call on specific players. For instance, if Player X moves his pivot foot without being caught, the league would send out a video featuring half a dozen players—including Player X—making that mistake, thereby sending a message to the refs: watch these specific players and their illegal habits.

Tim, this practice is called "Quality Control" and every good business has a system to check, monitor, and promote it.

In other words, move along. Nothing to see here.

Don't you think if the NFL saw that a particular tight end was gaining an unfair advantage by illegally using his hands to get open—outside the normal view of the referees—that the league would address it? They would be well within their rights to send out a memo stating, "This is happening. It needs to stop. Please be aware."

Again, common sense? You there? Anybody home?

This isn't cheating, Timmy. It's not a backhanded way to get the right teams to win the right games. Las Vegas casinos have employed similar methods to stem card counting and other nefarious activities at their tables.

Here's another Donaghy gem: if the league wanted a home team to win a big game, it would assign officials known to possess "rabbit ears"—guys who hear every catcall and fear verbal abuse. By Donaghy's reasoning, these guys would be less likely to call fouls on the home teams, which gives the home team an unseen advantage.

Once again, Donaghy's words are music to the ears of the conspiracy folks, but they don't hold up to a simple counterargument:

A. Wouldn't that referee have an issue with *any* game and not just "big" games in which the league had a stake in dictating the winner?

B. This isn't a league issue; it's a bad referee issue. Why concoct a conspiracy theory around something that happens because a referee is not good at his job?

In *Personal Foul,* Donaghy spills this secret: NBA officials would often play a game among themselves in which the official calling the first foul or infraction is declared the loser. This would result, of course, in referees—presumably only the ones who wanted to win this game-within-the-game—swallowing their whistles in the early moments.

Yes, that's unprofessional. No question. Unprofessional. Childish. Dumb. Pick your adjective.

But, in a regular season with roughly 3,700 fouls called over the course of more than 1,200 games, does anyone believe this brand of silliness would alter the power of the league?

Or even the outcome of a game?

In fact, I'll go one step further: since it doesn't intrinsically favor one team over another, it wouldn't even alter the score of that *quarter*.

Let's back up for a moment, extract ourselves from the thicket of brambles growing inside Donaghy's mind and return to one basic truth: Officials in all sports are human. They get caught up in special moments, they make mistakes under pressure, they are vulnerable to impatience and anger.

It should also be noted that leagues *do* want to protect their top performers from physical harm; that's why some rules are instituted to allow the most talented to flourish. Hockey, for instance, is simply a more attractive and consumable product if the most gifted skaters and scorers have the space to . . . you know . . . score and skate.

The NBA might take the most criticism for protecting its stars, but the NFL created a rule to protect quarterbacks that's universally accepted as "The Brady Rule." Tom Brady was lost for the 2008 season after a defensive player—already on the ground—lunged at Brady's knee and tore it up. A prized NFL asset was injured, and now hitting a quarterback below the waist when he's considered defenseless is a penalty.

Cheating, or just savvy business? I'm going with savvy business.

The truth is, an onrushing defensive end can't lunge at Peyton Manning's knee, but he also can't lunge at John Skelton's knee.

All leagues deal with charges of favoritism on some level. Longtime NHL reporter Larry Brooks of the *New York Post* claimed the Pittsburgh Penguins, owned by former superstar Mario Lemieux, were "made men" in the league, protected because of the status of their famous owner and the skills of current star Sidney Crosby.

But the NBA is far and away the leader when it comes to

suspicion. It's like listening to someone prattle on outside the Texas Schoolbook Depository: Wilt Chamberlain never fouled out of a game; Michael Jordan and Magic Johnson rarely fouled out; LeBron James went more than two weeks without being called for a foul.

Is this preferential treatment, or merely a statistical acknowledgment that better players are more agile and aggressive, capable of both avoiding and drawing more fouls?

LeBron was recently quoted as saying, "I've never fouled much, even back to high school." The man is 6 foot 9 inches and 250 pounds with less than 5 percent body fat and world-class fast-twitch muscles. Why is it hard to believe that he doesn't need to foul regularly to play great defense?

A recent academic study of NBA officiating detected biases, but not the ones you might expect. The study was conducted by three economic researchers, and it found little or no evidence that referees favor teams from larger media markets. It found, somewhat surprisingly, that teams trailing in a playoff game or series received the benefit of the calls.

Yes, Mr. Donaghy, NBA refs favored the little guys.

Those findings align with a 2009 study of college basketball officiating—authored by a professor from Ball State University and another from Indiana University's Kelley School of Business. Just like the NBA study, the NCAA study showed that a team trailing in a game is more likely to get the next call.

They're humans. They're vulnerable. They're influenced by emotions.

Donaghy felt differently. He believed his ability to pick games based on officiating habits was a sign the league dictated outcomes and determined eventual champions.

Well, Tim, I have a different take: you're simply a guy who had unique access to the league and the kind of information only the keenest eye can detect.

You were studying *human* patterns, not conspiracies.

Curt Schilling kept a book on umpires in an effort to use those human factors to his advantage. Nothing wrong with that. During the 2012 baseball season, Brian Runge was behind the plate for two of twelve no-hitters.

Uh-oh.

Cue the ominous horror-movie music.

There's got to be a conspiracy brewing, right?

I don't know—in 1990, Drew Coble called balls and strikes for two of seven no-hitters. In fact, there have been roughly 280 no-hitters thrown in the big leagues—eight umps have called four and nine have called three. Is it favoritism—even, dare we say it, *cheating* by the pitchers?—or simply the end result of umpires who tend to have larger strike zones?

Usually the least complicated and most likely answer is the correct one.

In other words, it's always good to remember Sutton's law:

If you hear hoofbeats behind you, think horses, not zebras.

49ers quarterback—and the face of the franchise—Colin Kaepernick wears a Miami Dolphins hat in public. It goes viral on Twitter and he predictably gets flack from some fans in San Francisco. Of course he would. To make it worse, he tells fans to get a life. You must be bored, he says.

It's just a hat, right? No big deal, right? Kaepernick still loves the 49ers, right?

Let me ask you this: You okay with your wife having her ex-boyfriend's name and face tattooed on her? It's just a tat, right? It's just ink, right? She still loves you, right?

There are these things called boundaries, and in this case the fans are right. They have a right to be ticked off. Kaepernick crossed a loyalty boundary.

Do you think it's cool for the president of Six Flags to wear Disney gear in public? If you ran Fox Sports, would you be happy with your employees wearing ESPN gear in public? I can hear you now—"Come on, Colin, those are rivals." Well, there are only thirty-two NFL teams, all vying for the same top free agents, coaches, scouts, and administrators. You don't have to be in somebody's division to be a rival.

You don't think Cowboys owner Jerry Jones views the Pittsburgh Steelers and New England Patriots, both in the AFC, as rivals? It's all market share, and Jones wants more of it.

Maybe the younger generation has grown up with fewer boundaries, and this is a blind spot. At some point in everyone's life, though, boundaries are needed.

Think about how we raise our kids. We set up boundaries for them constantly. We tell our children "Don't talk to strangers." Or "Never get into a car at school unless it's with Mom or Dad." Those aren't laws, just boundaries we set for safety.

Everyone's favorite athlete, Michael Jordan, was the all-time boundary-setter. The way MJ sees it, you are with him or against him. Remember during the Dream Team Olympics, after winning gold, he draped a flag over the Reebok logo to cover it. Why? He was a Nike guy. A loyalty boundary had been set.

Call me a shill. Call me a company man. I just believe I owe my employer and fellow employees some public loyalty. At least while we're in the trenches together.

Miami Heat team president Pat Riley dresses like a movie character who is playing the part of a man who dresses really well.

Conspiracy of Dunces

onspiracy theories are the best. Every major event seems to spawn a million nonofficial versions assembled from little bits and pieces of evidence that always add up to a cover-up or a huge lie. I'm fascinated by the theories and theorists—even when I know they're completely, outrageously out of their minds.

Why are these theories so damned fascinating? Simple: even the most implausible theory seems to carry enough truth to create doubt. One piece of information leads to another and pretty soon enough dots are connected to make even the most outlandish theory seem possible. The sadly delusional 9/11 Truthers, the believers in the Roswell alien invasion—they all manage to stumble upon something that leads to something bigger. By the time I walked out of the theater after seeing *JFK*, Oliver Stone almost had me buying into the Magic Bullet theory.

Sports haven't been spared the conspiracy bug. Conspiracy Guy in sports has been hanging around the fringes for years, picking up just enough credibility and followers to keep the conversation flowing. As a radio host, I find him annoying and tedious, someone who refuses to accept reason, and I feel I'm in a unique position to put my three most favorite conspiracy theories to bed.

It's the least I can do for America.

Conspiracy theorists in this country have their favorites: the UFOs of Roswell, New Mexico; the JFK assassination; Obama's birth certificate. What follows are my sports versions, the Mount Rushmore of sports conspiracy theories, fueled by irrational fandom and a willful adherence to cynicism over common sense.

The Frozen Envelope

This is my favorite. I love this one.

It goes like this: before the 1985 NBA draft, commissioner David Stern had the Knicks' lottery envelope frozen so he could feel it in the tumbler and pull it out only for the No. 1 pick, which would give New York the rights to draft Georgetown center Patrick Ewing, by far the best player in the draft.

The idea behind this theory—the kernel of "truth" that sprouts all the wild tendrils—is the age-old belief that sports leagues want big-market teams, especially New York teams, to be successful. A successful New York team, the theory goes, makes for a successful and profitable league.

This fails to address a central question: If the league wanted to ensure major-market superiority—and had the ability to manipulate events such as the draft to make it happen—can someone explain why New York has had decades in which its franchises were irrelevant? How about Boston, Philadelphia, Washington, D.C., both Los Angeles franchises? Why aren't they good all the time?

But what really gets me is the assumption that David Stern, a young star executive in one of the most high-profile positions in sports, would willingly risk his entire career to get Patrick Ewing in a Knicks uniform.

This man, who was once the executive counsel for the league, would throw away *everything*—including a seven-figure salary for decades ahead—to mastermind the biggest scandal since the 1919 Black Sox.

It's truly astounding.

Where's Stern's motivation in this? No commission has ever had a contract based on which markets win the most games. During his career, he's continuously had bigger and bigger contracts no matter who was winning. The Celtics, Knicks, Lakers—they've all been down during his tenure, and it hasn't affected him in the least. He was getting more money and more power when the league was headlined by Allen Iverson, Stephon Marbury, and Stevie Francis. Why should he care about Patrick Ewing?

There was absolutely no benefit for him to risk throwing away his entire career to help the Knicks be good. None at all.

Patrick Ewing became a Knick because that's the way it happened. The envelope wasn't frozen, and Stern didn't mastermind some bizarre conspiracy to elevate his league and himself by elevating the Knicks.

Common sense: the enemy of the conspiracy theorists.

UNLV's Tank Job

The 1991 national championship game between the UNLV Runnin' Rebels and the Duke Blue Devils was supposed to be a mismatch. The Rebels were riding a forty-five-game winning streak and had beaten Duke the year before in the title game by 30.

Duke didn't have a chance.

And yet Duke won.

There had to be something sinister at work, right? The losers were from Las Vegas, a place practically begging for conspiracy theories, so the Rebels' loss had to be a result of point shaving or some other nefarious gambling activity. In other words, they threw the game.

Conveniently, the conspiracy folks fail to acknowledge several important facts. Duke was loaded with good players—Grant Hill, Bobby Hurley, Christian Laettner—who put together a 30-5 record while playing in a far better conference than UNLV's. The Devils were making their fourth straight trip to the Final Four.

Hill, a freshman, wasn't around the year before and was emerging as a force.

Duke had the superior coach and the revenge factor on its side. UNLV was trying to become the first repeat champion since the 1972–73 UCLA Bruins. Set aside any bizarre notions of outside influences and ask yourself one question: Who do you think felt more pressure?

I was there, and Duke was on its game from the opening tip. The Devils also got the benefit of several close calls, including one that fouled out valuable UNLV point guard Greg Anthony.

But look: upsets happen. They happen often, and they happen even more often in the NCAA Tournament.

Is it so hard to believe that Duke was better than we thought, and UNLV not as good as we thought? Is it an impossibility to believe that UNLV came in tight and never got untracked? Couldn't I argue—with conviction—that Duke's big three of Laettner, Hill, and Hurley were better than UNLV's top three?

Unfortunately, conspiracies don't leave room for outlier events, such as Duke beating UNLV or an official making a terrible call in a crucial moment of a huge game. An unusual event always has to be dissected with a skeptical eye, paving the way for every nutcase to see the outrageous in the coincidental.

Because there's another archenemy of the conspiracy theory: coincidence.

Sometimes things just happen. No rhyme, no reason—they just do.

There are 14,000 airports in the United States and 80,000 individual flights a day. And yet, at least a handful of times a year I run into a colleague or a friend during a layover somewhere in the country. How is that even possible?

And here's something I've always wanted to know: Why do so many serial killers have the name "Lee"? There must be a reason, right? I've read a ton of books about serial killers—hey, they fascinate me, OK?—and it's uncanny how many Lees there are.

Forget JFK assassin Lee Harvey Oswald and Tucson shooter Jared Lee Loughner, who shot 19—including congresswoman Gabrielle Giffords—and killed six. Instead, let's limit the discussion to conventional serial killers.

The presumed Zodiac killer is Arthur Leigh Allen and the Green River killer is Gary Leon Ridgeway. The South Hill killer is Robert Lee Yates and the D.C. sniper is Boyd Lee Malvo. Henry Lee Lucas was once considered America's most prolific killer. Derrick Todd Lee was a serial-killing monster from Baton Rouge.

This is a phenomenon that spans continents. Bruce George Peter Lee was imprisoned on twenty-six charges of manslaughter in Great Britain in 1981.

Why? How? If you saddle your son with any form of *Lee*, are you automatically improving his odds of roaming the nation killing people? Or could it be something more innocent? Is it possible that *Lee* is a popular name among families from lower socioeconomic levels, which makes them more prone to abuse and their children more prone to violence later in life? Probably, but the mystery and dark nature of the unknown makes for a better story.

I admit the level of coincidence in the *Lee/serial killer* example is staggering, but there's nothing sinister or serious there. It's just a series of weird coincidences. Serial killers have long been a uniquely American fascination, and movies like *Silence of the Lambs* created a mini-industry of cable television shows, books, and amateur sleuths.

One of the first serial killers to achieve celebrity status—for lack of a better term—was Ted Bundy. He doesn't fit the mold of the stereotypical deranged madman. He attended the University of Washington, was affable and handsome. He even defended himself in court.

Theodore Robert Bundy breaks the "Lee" mold, too.

But wait. If you research the details of his arrest, you'll find that he was pulled over by a Pensacola, Florida, police officer. Bundy wrestled with the officer and got away briefly before being apprehended.

That cop's name?

David Lee.

The Bloody Sock

Game 6 of the 2004 American League Championship Series immediately became part of baseball lore. Red Sox starter Curt Schilling beat the Yankees while pitching with a torn tendon sheath in his right ankle that had been sutured in place by Red Sox doctors in a procedure that nobody could remember being done before. Late in the game, network cameras caught a growing spot of blood on Schilling's right sock, which sent the broadcast crew into seizures of hyperbole.

Schilling was courageous, bold, single-minded. He was a man's man, a team guy, a fearless warrior.

Boston was on its way to winning four straight against the Yankees after falling behind three games to none, and the end result of that postseason was the first Red Sox world championship since 1916.

So yeah, Schilling's ankle became a big deal.

Three years later, announcer Gary Thorne said he was told by former Boston catcher Doug Mirabelli that Schilling painted the sock to heighten the drama. This sent the conspiracy-minded into overdrive.

Where was the kernel of truth in this case? With Schilling, of course. He had developed a reputation as something of a self-promoter. He spoke his mind and wasn't universally beloved within the game.

The most common response to Mirabelli's alleged revelation was this:

If anyone would do this, it would be Schilling.

That probably wouldn't stand up in a court of law, but it was good enough for the guy who wants to believe nothing happens either organically or by chance.

Beyond the fact that Schilling has many detractors who would love to see his reputation take a hit, the claim has no basis.

Fact: The actual game sock is in the Baseball Hall of Fame and could be tested.

Fact: Doug Mirabelli denied he ever said what Thorne reported.

Fact: Thorne, sensing his credibility took a major hit, never discussed it again.

Fact: Schilling immediately offered $1 million to anyone who could prove it.

Fact: Schilling, like all Boston players, let the bottom of his pants hang low around his ankles, making it hard to spot the blood. If he was seeking attention, why not hike up the pants?

Fact: Team trainers have confirmed his injury was real and sutures were used.

Fact: Sutures often break and cause bleeding under duress.

Fact: A big part of pitching is leg drive, which could easily put tension on a pitcher's ankles, and Schilling was a classic drop-and-drive pitcher who used his legs to generate power.

More than anything, the bloody sock was the result of great camera work by the guys working for Fox.

Like the frozen envelope and Duke beating UNLV, Schilling's sock was just a strange but explainable instance of sports being sports.

Buster Douglas beat the unbeatable Mike Tyson and overcame 42-1 odds along the way. Everyone was shocked, but it turns out there were signs that something crazy could happen. Douglas's mother, Lula Pearl, had died three weeks earlier, motivating Buster to train harder in her memory. Tyson was heavier than usual and had recently parted with longtime trainer Kevin Rooney. Throw into the mix Tyson's combustible relationship with his wife at the time, Robin Givens, and the ingredients were there.

Adrenaline-filled, stress-free, motivated athletes—Buster Douglas, Curt Schilling, Grant Hill, Christian Laettner, and Bobby Hurley—often overachieve.

The single most baffling and unexplainable moment in American sports history has to be the "Miracle On Ice." A group of American hockey players, who had been humiliated the week before the 1980 Olympics by the Russians, 10-3, somehow beat the same USSR team and went on to win the gold medal. That Soviet team came into that game 27-1-1 since the 1960s in Olympic play, and the ragtag group of Americans was not considered a serious threat.

But wonderful, crazy, wild, and unpredictable things happen.

At the end of the game, Al Michaels famously asked, "Do you believe in miracles?"

Yes I do, Al, yes I do.

But don't mistake that for gullibility—there are many things I *don't* believe in. And that list starts with—but is not limited to—frozen envelopes, tank jobs, and fake blood seeping through a white sock.

Whenever I hear the term *control freak*, it makes me think we should come up with another term—or at least another category—for strong, willful people in control. Something with a little more positive spin. It just seems like many of these supposed control freaks are actually pretty good at turning around companies or businesses.

The late technology whiz Steve Jobs was a control freak, wasn't he? It certainly seems that way if you read his biography. He wanted a say in everything Apple was creating, and in the end the consumer won. Sometimes feelings would be hurt, but tension and disagreement are often part of any creative process.

Think about all those crazy control freaks in football. Bill Belichick of the Patriots and Jim Harbaugh of the 49ers would be one and two on any NFL-control-freak list. Belichick won't even allow his assistants to talk to the media. They also happen to be, quite possibly, the two best head coaches in the league.

Nick Saban of Alabama and Urban Meyer of Ohio State also own reputations as almost maniacal behind-the-scenes leaders. Nothing happens at either school until both coaches have a final say. They override assistants on the smallest matter without guilt. Aren't they considered the two best college football coaches in the country?

Anytime you read a business book about turning a losing culture into a winning one they always talk about a need for attention to detail. It all starts with that. The best CEOs are lauded for it. Yet how do you know and manipulate every detail, in any rapidly changing business, without seizing control of a department or an idea that's under you? Is that a freak or is it a progressive boss willing to adjust on the fly and having the ability to spot small problems before they become big ones?

Why shouldn't a more experienced and frankly superior football intellect like Belichick override a less experienced and less talented assistant coach? All coaches aren't equal. Neither are all technology employees at Apple.

Let's face the truth about control. We all like it when we have it and we mostly resent it or fear it when we don't.

It's different in personal relationships, where harmony often supersedes production. You're not competing against other couples. You're rarely on a deadline to get an argument resolved. Needing control creates resentment, which often creates a trip to divorce court.

But in business and certainly football, I want the smartest coach who is willing to occasionally hurt some feelings to get it right. If assistants are offended, then get new assistants. Belichick seems to win with a revolving door of assistants and coordinators. To me, he's a *control maven*, not a freak.

Sometimes you have to crush dreams, even of nine-year-olds: look at your dad; if he's 5 foot 2, you're not playing in the NBA.

Primal Time

Years ago I was approached by a radio executive who had grown tired and disgusted by a brand of on-air dialogue he considered too angry and mean. Rush Limbaugh was dominating the national airwaves with his now-familiar style of firebrand conservatism, and local markets—eager to capitalize on the ratings—were attempting to clone their own versions of Limbaugh.

This radio executive was offering me an afternoon slot as a general talk-show host to leave sports talk. He felt my socially liberal views would combat the evil forces of right-wing talk radio and right-wing politics.

I had a different opinion of Limbaugh. He didn't bother me, and I didn't see him as a threat to the radio industry or the nation. His anthem doesn't work for me, no matter how often he repeats it. I felt his popularity, and the popularity of his message, was wildly exaggerated.

When the executive told me he felt I could be a formidable counter to Limbaugh, I said, "You do realize that Bill Clinton is on his second term and he's wildly popular, right? People listen to political radio for affirmation, not information. Rush isn't changing minds or views—he's just reaffirming them."

The job offer flattered me, but the job didn't interest me. Moreover, I didn't think the executive's logic was valid. I left him with four words: "Don't worry about it."

Limbaugh was one of the first, but by no means is he the last. Even today, conservatives dominate talk radio. Fox News still maintains a massive following, but the GOP is falling further behind in presidential elections.

Why? How is this possible?

Popularity shouldn't be confused with influence. The media, as a whole, has less impact than politicians, public-relations staffs, and radio executives believe. There's a reason that people call those conservative talk shows hosted by Limbaugh, Sean Hannity, and Glenn Beck "The Echo Chamber." People listen and regurgitate what they hear, making the noise louder than it is meaningful.

Limbaugh's power comes from his narrative. He makes conservatives feel he has their backs, which gives him virtually no impact outside of a self-contained group that is already predisposed to believe what he says.

He's not changing minds. He's not making voters think twice about their political beliefs. There's so much anger and vitriol between the two sides that many people would consider it a personal failing—a refutation of who they are—to switch sides and vote for someone from the "enemy" camp.

What Limbaugh offers is connectivity, the personal reinforcement for people out there to know someone else thinks the way they do. His ability to create an enemy—the mainstream media—was a stroke of genius. The us-against-them mentality forges loyalty. And when it's packaged as a hardy band of underdogs (conservatives) fighting a monolithic force (the liberal media)? Hell, even better.

It's the Letterman vs. Leno dynamic. I have a friend, Tim Kelleher, who interned for Letterman, and he said their goal was to make the audience feel they were in on the joke. There's always been an inside-the-rope-line quality to Letterman's show that you don't get from Leno. The loyalty is generated by the fact that not everyone gets the joke. And a Letterman joke that bombs—strangely—still ends up working.

There's a similar principle at work in sports. Leagues and teams fret over negative publicity or—even worse—irrelevance.

Negative publicity at least gets your name out there. Being ignored is a death sentence.

Oftentimes, these teams and leagues argue that they're producing a good product. This misses the point. Like Limbaugh, they need a narrative to lead the way.

The MLS or NHL might feel neglected, but I'm here to tell them a cruel truth:

It's not us. It's you.

Tell a better story. Get more compelling stars, or do a better job telling us about the ones you already have. Give us a reason to be excited about your sport and we'll be there.

Conveniently, there's a perfect blueprint out there for all you underserved sports to follow: MMA.

There's no plausible reason for this sport to exist, let alone thrive. Best-case scenario, it should be stumbling down a hospital hallway with frantic nurses on each side and a priest in tow. It has survived obstacles and setbacks that would have destroyed even the best-financed and most shrewdly promoted enterprise.

Think about it. The sport didn't even have a legitimate *name* until ten years after it started. It was called various forms of "cage fighting" until it was called No Holds Barred, which sounds like a cross between a bad hairspray and a Guns N' Roses ballad. Not that long ago, the only places fights could be legally staged were on Indian reservations, which meant most of its events were held in remote spots in the mountains outside San Diego or the Central Valley.

When the sport finally settled on the more valuable MMA label, it had to change some of its most popular rules to reduce violence and make itself more palatable to a wider audience. In effect, MMA had to eliminate some of the elements that made a certain segment of the population like it in the first place.

Once it fought its way into the public consciousness and earned a spot on pay-per-view cable, senator John McCain led a successful push to throw it off the air. McCain didn't like its viciousness and vulgarity and coined the term "human cockfighting" to describe it.

Yet popularity soared.

Cage fighting was virtually ignored by the mainstream media, which usually mentioned it only to disparage it. To watch the best fights, fans have to pay separately; to watch the lesser fights, fans have to find the channel that falls between Lithuanian ballet and the Montana Wood-Carving Championship.

Yet popularity soared.

It had a primary rival—boxing—which had something in the neighborhood of a hundred-year head start. It's still barred in New York, America's largest city. It has very few true "name" stars, and its participants don't come through the ranks in high-profile college programs, like football and basketball.

And yet—you guessed it—popularity soars.

How? Why?

Under Dana White, the UFC connected with fans. It created an underground renaissance built on anticorporate bravado. It developed an image of a dark, secret league that only insiders understood. The loyalty this generated was incredible.

White tells a really, really good story, and he understands the power of narrative. He has created storylines and rivalries, with humble, everyman stars who don't command extreme salaries. The sport sells a brand of affordable sex appeal that attracts members of both sexes in the targeted youth demographic.

UFC isn't flourishing because it suddenly picked up massive amounts of media support. You don't read long, detailed stories about its championship bouts in the *New York Times*. In fact, they've used that to their advantage, too. The lack of media attention has created a revolutionary feel to the sport—screw the rest of you, this is *my* sport.

Like most people my age who grew up with the mainstream sports, I was highly skeptical of cage fighting when I first laid eyes on it in 1995. I was in San Francisco at the end of a long night with friends when we walked into a bar called The Condor. Dark and rough, it was the perfect place to experience what was beaming down at us from several big screens.

At this point, the sport wasn't called MMA. In my mind, it could have easily been named WHW, for What the Hell Am I Watching?

It was a series of raw, uncomfortably violent fights. Eye gouging was permitted, and I can only hope the American Optometrists Association lodged a formal complaint. It was the sort of scene I can imagine seeing in a rural tavern at 2 a.m. the night of a plant closure. Or maybe in the parking lot of a Raider game.

I watched, but I was disgusted.

Nearly two decades later, the sport is not only standing but punching back.

My bad.

White's efforts have tapped into a vein of American sports fan who doesn't find much to like in baseball, basketball, and football. They connect to the anarchist mentality of MMA. It's back to the insider idea; they're getting something they can't get somewhere else. They draw strength from knowing there are other people out there like them. Watching UFC and wearing TapOut gear is like nodding along to Limbaugh or laughing at one of Letterman's failed jokes.

The success of MMA—and specifically the UFC—proves the customer is always right. The marketplace dictates success and failure. Sports networks have promoted women's basketball, college baseball, the Tour de France, and rodeo, but those audiences remain small. Ultimate fighting, however, exploded in popularity without the benefit of a "sugar daddy" network or even a popular proponent among newspaper columnists. The sport was virtually ignored when it wasn't being singled out for ridicule or elimination.

Through the years, the sport blew through every major disadvantage.

The critics haven't disappeared. They feel the sport has blossomed only on the strength of bloodlust. Violence sells, right? Then why isn't hockey more popular? Why has boxing basically vanished?

Simple: MMA survived, and thrived, because it made people care. It connected with its core audience and made it feel important and special. It sold a grassroots narrative that a lot of people on the fringes identified with.

I don't have to love or even regularly consume a product to respect its path to popularity. The rise of MMA, over and through countless obstacles, highlights a bigger and more inspirational story: people with ideas and passion overcome the roadblocks that are placed in front of them. The defining quality is passion, not fancy titles or bloated ad campaigns or celebrity endorsers.

Starbucks overcame the Great Recession not by slashing prices or ramping up a fancy television campaign but by speeding up service and touting a have-it-your-way Frappuccino. My mom and dad didn't get in the car and drive somewhere to get their cup of Folgers, but millions feel their days aren't complete without their 9 a.m. and 4 p.m. Starbucks runs.

Great ideas and great thinkers can thrive in the worst economy and against the longest odds. The UFC is proof.

So all of you sports leagues and teams whining about lack

of media coverage need to look to Dana White and MMA for an example of how to make it work.

Tell a better story. Cast yourself as a revolutionary or an underdog. Connect with your constituents. Make them believe you're giving them something they can't get anywhere else.

Listen to Dana White.

Or, if all else fails, Rush Limbaugh.

Hockey is never going to be as popular in this country as football or basketball. It didn't originate here, and it's just so much better in person than on television. Probably comparable to Broadway. You can only really feel it if you're there.

But the sport doesn't do itself any favors with marketing. When they returned after the strike, the ad campaign they sold to the public was, "Hockey is back."

Now, think about that. You are reminding us that you left. Reminding fans of your labor strife.

"Hey fans, we may have ticked you off. We realize you're the most loyal fans in sports. But listen, we are back. Now. Today. What's up?"

Brilliant.

This is a sport with so many assets. It has great parity and good-looking players who play through injuries. There're very few divas and, unlike most pro sports, it's mostly relatable dudes. The sport is also superfast with a regulated level of violence. Many major cities such as Boston, New York, Detroit, Chicago, and Philadelphia love the sport. Yet can most sports fans name four players?

Introduce me to those guys.

Be demographic specific in your ads. Sell young people and maybe women. Sell a party, not just the sport. It's how Mark Cuban turned around the Dallas Mavericks. Invite the sexiest girls in town. The guys will follow.

Let the party begin. Get the ten best-looking guys in the league, splice in some hard checks, some great goals. Sell the speed of the game. This is what real men play. You can't turn the channel even if you dislike hockey. Let me see the fans. Hockey fans are nuts. Add some hip music and remember, you are selling a vibe, not just a sport.

Then have those guys look straight into a camera and say, "Ladies, we're in town this week. We're having a party. Bring some of your friends."

Fade to black. White letters then appear. "The party is back. Bring your friends."

Now that is a place I want to hang out. Stop reminding me you dumped me and broke my heart.

The marketing campaign says, "What happens in Vegas stays in Vegas." I disagree. What happens in Las Vegas—tell everyone you know. What happens in Dayton, Ohio, keep to yourself. Nobody cares.

Bean There, Done That

I f you're anything like me, parenting is one continuous real-ity check. When your son is five, you think he could become President of the United States. By six you're hoping he could be president of a fraternity and by seven you're awake nights pray-ing he doesn't end up on a grainy security tape on the eleven o'clock news.

The ups and downs are tough. I've also come to realize I'm much more forgiving of my kids than I might be of, say, *your* kids. Mine just make common, age-appropriate mistakes—*phases,* let's call them—while your kids are completely undisciplined and prob-ably need counseling.

My philosophy pretty much boils down to this: I love my kids; I tolerate yours.

I have high hopes for my kids, and I'll defend them to the death. Come to think of it, I'm a lot like Boston, the most peculiar and parochial sports city in America.

Fans in every city have emotional connections to their teams. There's no debating that. But as I have discovered, Boston takes it a step further. A *big* step.

I was first hired by ESPN ten years ago, and I made a simple request to get television ratings for every market for every event, large or small.

Immediately, one truth became undeniable: Boston is, with-out debate, the most provincial major market in the country.

Rose Bowl? Not interested.

Indy 500? Crickets.

Final Four? Final *What*?

I'm not here to claim Chicago loves NASCAR or New York is a college football Mecca, but Boston's ratings were a healthy notch below the norm for every major event that didn't include a Boston-area team.

I can hear it now. Every Fitzy or Patrick O'Connor on the South End is hollering, "So what? This ain't a college town. All we care about are pro sports."

Fine, but the same argument could be made for several major cities—Chicago, Minneapolis, San Francisco, Dallas—where they still watch nonlocal teams far more often. Boston, judging by the numbers, is a world all its own.

Why? Is it geographical? Boston's tucked up in a corner of the country with no connection to the rest of the nation. Am I supposed to believe that? I'm supposed to believe that one of the most educated cities in the world doesn't get cable TV or the Internet? Does the Red Zone Channel fail to penetrate New England? For a quick comparison, take Honolulu. It's a city with quite a bit of outdoor entertainment. It's not exactly rubbing elbows with Iowa. And yet it's the highest-rated NFL market without a team. Sorry, Tommy Boy, the count's now 0-2.

The numbers I found most surprising were World Series ratings. We all know Boston as a hub of baseball history and enthusiasm. But explain this: from 2010 to 2012, a three-year span, World Series ratings in Boston were substantially lower than most major markets. They were even lower than many markets without major-league franchises.

How can that be? Boston *is* baseball, right?

Nope. It just loves its own kids.

Judging sports towns can be tricky. Los Angeles has a terrible reputation. It's the place where fans arrive late and leave early. It's apathetic. It's dependent on trends and glamour and who's hot now. But going through the last five years of attendance figures, the Dodgers and Angels outdrew the Yankees and Mets in four of them, with the fifth being a draw. Those numbers have to include a significant notation: during that time the Dodgers were owned by the slippery Frank McCourt, who was so despised that many Dodger fans protested his ownership in the final year by refusing to attend games.

For the most part, we have a grasp on the cities that occupy the pantheon of sports fandom. The exception is Boston, which gets high marks despite not seeming to care about anything outside its immediate vicinity.

I'm trying to figure this out. These kinds of sociological oddities fascinate me, and I've come up with two possible roadblocks Boston faces when it comes to caring about anything past its nose.

1. Boston is too smart: an article titled "Us vs. America," which used polling information from Northeastern University, made the case that Boston is simply different than most major cities. It's more liberal, for one, which makes it more tolerant than the national average on issues such as gay marriage, abortion rights, and interracial sex. It has less gun ownership and less violence. Its population is younger, smokes less, and works out more. It's home to more than seventy universities and colleges, eight of them major research universities. Those are staggering numbers.

In addition, Boston is a financial, health care, and banking hub. The city and its surrounding areas are full of educated and busy people who have many interests and the disposable income to pursue those interests.

Under that scenario, watching *your* team doesn't make the cut.

2.   History—and not just sports history: forget for a moment the Celtics' seventeen NBA titles, the Bruins' six Stanley Cups, the coolest ballpark ever built, and Tom Brady. Let's talk *real* history.

Boston loves itself just a little more than any other city. If you were born and educated there, maybe you would, too.

Sports allegiances tend to emerge at around nine or ten years old, when kids are aware enough to understand the rules of the games and old enough to replicate those games in the backyard.

It also coincides with the time kids begin learning about American history in school. This is yet another way Boston is different. The American Revolution, which created many of our political and social beliefs, took place almost exclusively in and around Boston. The Boston Tea Party, the Battle of Bunker Hill, the midnight ride of Paul Revere—I learned about all of these events at an early age, but they took place somewhere else.

Not if you're a Boston kid, though. If you're a Boston kid, all of those events were home games.

If the seminal events in your nation's history took place in your backyard, you'd probably get the sense that your city is special. Seriously, the birthplace of the country was right down the block—how cool is that? Field trips are a who's who of founding fathers and profoundly important historical sites.

So many of the names that are synonymous with America hail from the city. Ben Franklin, John Quincy Adams, and Edgar Allan Poe provide the foundation, and by seventh grade you're listening to Mrs. Hathaway discuss the Kennedys. All Boston-bred. Hometown heroes. If you spent your entire childhood being told—directly or indirectly—that you're special and different and just a little bit better than everybody else, wouldn't you start to believe it?

Seriously, even when Bostonians vacation they do it in their backyard. From Cape Cod to Nantucket to Martha's Vineyard, Massachusetts is home to some of the country's most sought-after summer refuges.

Maybe some of this will help explain why most surveys of least-friendly cities find Boston near the top. The word *smug* tends to come up. If you live in New England, the term *Mass-holes* is a familiar, if ugly, one. The city sees itself as more important, more informed, and more historically relevant. The people who live there consider themselves descendants of American royalty. And in some ways, they're right.

Boston is America's five-year-old, primed to be president.

It views itself as different, special—perhaps even better than you.

And it sees your teams as monumentally unimportant.

When you make money out West you earn the right *not* to wear a tie. Out East you just buy a nicer tie.

The Gracious Host

One of the by-products of our celebrity-soaked culture is a tendency to rely on the grandiose, mythical tale. The idea of one all-knowing messiah leading the uninitiated to safety through the churning waters of doubt is a staple of our time. Steve Jobs—and Steve Jobs alone—led Apple's renaissance. The power of Ronald Reagan's personality was the sole factor in reenergizing a sagging economy. Billy Beane's ability to see beyond standard baseball statistics single-handedly turned the small-market Oakland Athletics into a contender.

These stories make best sellers and cinematic fortunes, but their appeal has simple roots: they're easier to tell than the layered truth. Rarely does one person or one idea or one factor turn around a country or a business or a team. The truth is found in the convergence of many factors.

Similarly, the NFL's current momentum and popularity is based on more than Roger Goodell's leadership. It is a factor, sure, but there are almost too many others to count: a healthy connection to gambling in an increasingly gambling-centric nation; a level of controlled violence; a tech-friendly mentality; a pace and composition that's made for television; and admirable parity.

That last one might be oversold by the media, but it's true nonetheless. Set against baseball's deep-pocketed aristocracy and the NBA's invitation-only glamour society, there is a sense that an NFL team can succeed wildly with the right coach and the right quarterback.

From Rust Belt to Sun Belt, from Left Coast to Right Coast, you can win anywhere served by Google Maps. The NFL just feels a little more fair, even for the smallest of franchises. Green Bay has no owner and one hotel of significance within its city limits, and yet the Packers have thirteen league championships and four Super Bowl titles.

Parity. Balance. Even. Equal. Fair. The NFL does a better job of either creating that reality or making us feel like it's pretty close to the truth.

So with that said, why wouldn't the NFL consider a daring but reasonable way to alter the way some games are decided?

Hear ye, hear ye—the esteemed court of Cowherd does declare that initial overtime possessions, from this point forward, will all go to the visitors. Out with the coin! Off with its freshly minted head!

In 2012, the NFL changed its overtime policy. It used to be sudden death—first score wins. Now it's sudden death with a disclaimer: first score wins, providing it's a touchdown. If it's just a field goal, the other fellas get a shot, too.

This change wasn't made to protect players—there was no safety issue.

This change wasn't made to protect the league's assets—there was no financial gain involved.

The NFL did it because ninety-one years after the first professional football game, even the smartest people in the sport struggle with how to make the overtime period truly fair.

Just take a look at overtime periods across all levels of football. College and high school football use something called a Kansas Playoff, which seems cool on the surface but has the potential to become a time-consuming mess. Each team gets at least one possession from a predetermined spot on the field, and the possession ends when a team scores, misses a field goal, or turns the ball over. If the score remains tied after each team gets a possession, they do it again. If the score is tied after the second round of possessions, they do it again. If the score is tied after the third . . . basically, the Kansas Playoff can go on all night, with the brevity of a Senate hearing. Arkansas and Mississippi played seven overtimes a decade ago. Call it *Mississippi Burn-out* and be happy they're not charging by the hour for parking.

But is that truly a fair way to determine a winner? A series of possessions in the cluttered red zone? Doesn't the team with the better quarterback have a significant edge over a running team? Doesn't the home team have a decided edge since the end zones are generally the loudest places for opposing offenses to operate?

The NFL used sudden death for decades, starting in the mid-'70s. And then it decided a fairer way of determining a winner after four quarters was to kinda-sorta give each team a possession.

But if the NFL is concerned with parity—and it seems to believe parity is good for business—then why not *always* give the road team possession and call the first team that scores the winner?

From 1974 until the 2012 rule change, the first team with the ball won roughly 60 percent of the time. It's an edge, but not an overwhelming edge. It's perfectly understandable considering both defenses are bound to be worn down after sixty minutes of football. But that 60 percent figure is not extreme enough to indicate that a team with inferior talent would regularly win just on the basis of a favorable coin toss. A more truthful assessment is this: if you are reasonably efficient with the ball, you're better off getting the ball first.

And that's precisely the kind of slight variable that adds fairness for a road team facing the challenges of coming into a hostile venue.

Listen, football is the only sport where the crowd can hinder the opposing team's offense. When you see the home quarterback near the goal line using both arms to quiet the home crowd, that's actually sign language for, "It's a lot easier to run an efficient offense in this league when all of you 67,800 people don't make it sound like I'm standing inside a jet engine."

Every opposing team has to deal with that for every single one of their twelve to thirteen possessions. It's a true disadvantage that you don't find in any other sport. Opposing batters or pitchers aren't influenced negatively by noise. Field-goal percentages in the NBA aren't noticeably higher for the home team. But in the NFL, a sport increasingly built around the performance of the quarterback, there is real crowd adversity for the visiting team on each possession.

How do you quantify this? By looking at the home-road records of some of the all-time great quarterbacks. Terry Bradshaw was an astounding 70-15 at home and 41-42 on the road. Dan Marino was a stallion in South Beach, winning 83 of 121. On the road? More like a pony—65-57. Joe Namath had a losing road record while Matt Ryan is nearly unbeatable (33-5) in the Georgia Dome.

Clearly, the location of the game matters for quarterbacks. Why not even things out a little?

Why not give the road quarterback the ball first and return to the sudden-death format? It provides just a slight statistical edge in a league determined to make things more fair.

Let's put this in context. Every single thing in football is geared to favor the home team. The home team gets more practice time because it doesn't have to travel, a factor that grows with the greater distance the road team must travel. West Coast teams traveling east for early games (1 p.m. Eastern) are actually playing at 10 a.m. according to their body clocks. Home teams get more film time in a sport that values film more than Martin Scorsese and Francis Ford Coppola combined. We can even forget the benefits of sleeping and eating at home—those are obvious and part of every sport—but football is a film and preparation industry. There's one game a week, which makes preparation and superior coaching paramount.

Football is different that way. Basketball games are determined by the performance of star players. Baseball is about pitching. But football has evolved into a sport of coaching, and the salaries reflect as much. A college football coach, often working in a rural town and coaching just twelve games, earns an average of more than $1.6 million annually, according to *USA Today*. But a big-league manager working in a major metropolitan area managing 162 games averages less. In fact, sixteen big-league managers earn less than a million dollars a year. Why? Because coaching matters more in football, so it stands to reason that giving a coach more time to coach over the course of a week can be critical. That's one reason why top coaches with top quarterbacks are tough to beat at home.

So, long story short: playing at home is a considerable advantage for an NFL team.

The NFL's drafting, scheduling, and free-agency guidelines suggest a league that is consumed with fairness. The worst teams get the best draft picks and all that, so why not employ this one small change to acknowledge the inherent unfairness that comes with being an NFL team playing away from home? Why not at least give a small, subtle tip of the cap to the road team?

Just be a gracious host. Is that too much to ask?

We used to tell people with problems to "look in the mirror." Well, mirrors still work. We just don't use them anymore.

The Sport That Shouldn't Be

Take a look at a Q-tips box. Nowhere does the text tell you to jam those things in your ears, even though everybody—especially the people who make and market Q-tips—knows we all jam them in our ears. But on the box it tells you to use them to remove makeup, lipstick, nail polish. It doesn't say a word about your ear, except to tell you *not* to jam a Q-tip in your ear. This is basic legal protection.

The sports connection? Believe it or not, Q-tips and the X Games have something in common. For protection—legal and otherwise—the X Games should never, ever label itself a sport. In fact, the X Games should go out of its way to distance itself from mainstream sports, and it should start by getting all the X Games events out of the Olympics.

Here's why:

X Games events are adventure and should be marketed that way. At its heart, the X Games is a series of stunts—not a sport. There's no league, no commissioner, no officials. There are very few guidelines.

It's bullfighting, skydiving, cliff diving—one of many competitions built on risk and risk alone.

In real sports, risk is bad. A quarterback who puts himself at risk by going headfirst instead of sliding? Bad move. In the NHL, penalties are a risk that hurts a team. Baseball is a sport of percentages, where you play by the book 90 percent of the time. Risk in baseball often means losing.

The essence of the X Games boils down to this: *I can be a bigger badass than you.*

Risk is stardom. To be the next star, you have to do something more outrageous than the guy who came before you. You have to eclipse his *risk*. That's the key to the whole thing. It's the engine that keeps the machine running.

The object is to maintain the highest risk with artistic merit.

Entertainment.

Not sport.

Mike Trout doesn't have to eclipse anybody's risk. Neither does Aaron Rodgers or Kyrie Irving or the next great hockey star.

These kids in the X Games aren't Mike Trout or Aaron Rodgers or Kyrie Irving—they're the modern-day equivalent of Evel Knievel. Without the inevitable escalation of risk, there's no X Games.

The downside to this is obvious. Stunts go wrong, and when they do . . . damn, you're going to have major injuries. You're going to have deaths. These are realities that can't be avoided. They're built into the definition of what these events are. When snowmobiler Caleb Moore died after he crashed from what looked like about 200 feet in the air—on a snowmobile!—it was two things:

A tragic event.

And a by-product of the X Games culture.

But look what happened: the mainstream sports media took to the airwaves and the keyboards to decry Moore's death. It was reported in much the same way it might be reported if a soccer player or a speed skater had died. One problem: *it wasn't a death in a sporting event*.

Doesn't make it any less tragic. It just makes it more understandable.

It's a problem of classification.

Back to the Q-tips box: calling the X Games *sport* is equivalent to the folks at Q-tips putting *Stick this in your ear* right on the box. You don't want to make yourself susceptible to mainstream columnists and mainstream media. Nobody on the sports page talks about bullfighters dying, or WWE guys dying. There's a simple reason why: they're not branded as sports. They're either branded as entertainment or daredevils.

Traditional media members are typically men in their forties and fifties. They see sports as spectators. Most 17- to 21-year-olds see sports as participatory. This goes double or triple for the X Games—most traditional media people don't get it, and they aren't interested unless something horrible happens.

Get into the psyche of a 20-year-old kid. Society is far more corrosive than it was thirty years ago. I'll watch YouTube videos of a skateboard crash and wince. My 16-year-old stepson will watch them and laugh. There are entire television shows devoted to people having horrific crashes on skateboards. The 17- to 27-year-olds who are growing up in a more corrosive society with harsher images have a different stomach for the risks of X Games, and the injuries of X Games.

They're not offended by it. I am, but I'm old-school media. I shouldn't matter.

The mainstream media? Out of touch generationally on the X Games. But if you eliminate the branding, you solve the problem. They'll simply ignore it. Problem solved.

If I ran ESPN and the X Games, I would say never label it as sports in any promo again. And take every one of my events out of the Olympics.

Wrestling got kicked out of the Olympics at the beginning of 2013 and everybody associated with the sport was crestfallen. The X Games should get the hell out of the Olympics—as fast as possible—and then throw a major X Game–style party to celebrate.

I'm not suggesting they change the X Games. It's a huge success. Instead, change how it's categorized. It's like *tapas*. Are they an appetizer or an entree? They're both, they're neither—who knows? They're great, but the classification problem is why the local tapas restaurant will never be more popular than the Italian joint or the Mexican place.

Evel Knievel wasn't an athlete in the traditional sense. He was on *Wide World of Sports* when I was a kid but we never thought of him the way we thought of Walter Payton or Mike Schmidt or Kareem Abdul-Jabbar. If he got seriously injured, the mainstream sports media didn't jump up and down and call for a ban on motorcycle jumps or rocket rides across the Snake River Canyon. He was a guy performing a stunt.

Knievel bragged about breaking every bone in his body. That made him a hero. Broken bones are a badge of honor in very few human endeavors and precisely zero sports. Imagine an athlete in any sport bragging about broken bones or concussions or serious injuries. What general manager would say, "Hey, give me *that* guy"?

Of course not. Knievel would use it as a pitch to sponsors, and X Games performers take pride in their injuries because doing so is a testament to their willingness to take a risk. A fully intact body means you aren't going far enough.

If you aren't failing, you aren't trying.

There's only one logical conclusion: any linkage between the X Games and mainstream sports is simply an invitation to criticisms and lawsuits. It is the only "sport" that should never, under any circumstances, issue credentials to the mainstream media.

In fact, the media strategy of the X Games when it comes to mainstream sports media should consist of three words:

Please ignore us.

If X Games events continue to be part of the Olympics, they're going to be judged by the standards imposed by 50-year-old white guys who don't get it. And let's be clear about one thing: the Olympics needs the X Games events far more—*far* more—than the

X Games needs the Olympics. The X Games already has the network platform—ESPN. Most winter sports are dying for network support.

Without the Olympics, luge doesn't exist.

Downhill skiing needs the Olympics. Bobsledding needs the Olympics. The X Games has no need for the Olympics.

Conversely, X Games events are the best thing ever for the Olympics. What better way to attract a younger, hipper, cooler audience than to sandwich the snowboard halfpipe in between women's figure skating and speed skating?

A spot in the Olympics comes with legitimacy, whether it's earned or not and whether it's wanted or not.

Q-tips says, *Don't jam this in your ear.*

The X Games should say, *Don't ever confuse me with a sport.*

Get out. Get out of sports and get out of the Olympics. The sooner, the better.

Eddie Murphy was once the funniest person on the planet—then he decided he would rather be cool. Suddenly he was as funny as re-siding your house. Entourages and bodyguards take the air out of a punch line.

Good-looking isn't funny. Neither is 5 percent body fat.

Funny is disheveled, chunky, uncomfortable. It's living in Yonkers crammed in a house with too many people and too few rooms. New York City is funny because it's crowded and often miserably cold. You stay married in New York and fight through your problems. Los Angeles isn't funny because it's warm and spread out. People have space. They get divorced and start over and get happy again. Nothing ruins a knee-slapper like being content.

I was watching that show from years ago on NBC called *Last Comic Standing* when it dawned on me. The better weather the city had where that particular competition was being held, the lamer the comedians were. Boston or Minneapolis comics were gold. Phoenix Guy was a channel-turner. You really think the fact that Canada has given us dozens of hysterical people—and Australia virtually none—is just a coincidence?

Discomfort creates humor.

It's why I think most top comedians have roughly a ten- to twelve-year period to be labeled funniest guy on the planet. Then they become popular, rich, comfortable, and just another dude with a better sense of humor than most people.

Steve Martin, Chevy Chase, Bill Murray, David Letterman, Mike Myers, Jim Carrey, Ben Stiller, Chris Rock, Will Ferrell, and Jerry Seinfeld have all taken turns being that guy.

Eventually they all lose that slight edge after their third six-thousand-square-foot vacation home.

Someone please beg Zach Galifianakis and Aziz Ansari not to buy a Lexus.

USC and Alabama don't have a story like "Rudy." They would never have anybody that slow on the roster.

Southern Exposure

Everybody has an uneasy relationship with dynasties in American sports. We love to see them so we can either root for them or against them, and everybody feels equally strongly on one side or the other. We always associate dynasties with teams: Yankees, Lakers, Celtics, Steelers, Patriots. But right now, the biggest dynasty in American sports is a football conference.

And yes, there's no doubt about it: the SEC is a full-blown dynasty.

We understand this on a certain basic level. It's not that hard. We know SEC teams are 9-0 since the advent of the BCS Championship Games in 1998. We know they've won seven straight. We know that most of those games have featured dominating performances by the winning SEC team.

But it's my contention that we don't fully understand the depth of that dynasty. We don't understand the extent of the gap between SEC football and the rest of the conferences.

Let's break it down. By consensus, the second-best conference is the Big 12. We take this as an article of faith. The Pac 12 is finesse, the Big Ten is slow, but the Big 12 is the closest thing we have to legitimate competition for the SEC. The Big 12 sounds big and it sounds good. Texas vs. Oklahoma and all that.

So let's take a look at the one game in the season when we know we're going to get an SEC-Big 12 matchup: the Cotton Bowl. It's not a BCS game, so the Cotton Bowl has to wait until the BCS teams are decided before choosing one team from the SEC West and one team from the Big 12. It's often the third-place team in the SEC West against the second-place team in the Big 12.

Whatever the case, look at the last ten Cotton Bowls. Starting with the 2004 Cotton Bowl, when Ole Miss beat Oklahoma State, and ending with Texas A&M's rout of Oklahoma in 2013, the SEC has won nine of ten. The average score in those nine wins is 30-17, meaning the SEC team is nearly two touchdowns better.

And as they say on the infomercials, *But wait, there's more.*

For people who say the SEC's dominance is a little over-stated, think about this: the Chip Kelly Era in Oregon produced not only the highest-scoring offense in college football but a run-ning game that—in results if not style—harkens back to Nebraska in the '60s and '70s, or Oklahoma under Barry Switzer. In other words, it's a tour de force offense that everyone assumes is virtually unstoppable.

In 2010, the year Oregon reached the BCS title game, it aver-aged 41 points per game and ran for almost 3,500 yards. The Ducks were good—so good that they were pulling their starters at the half in the majority of their games. If they hadn't, it's reasonable to assume Oregon could have tacked on another 2,000 yards rushing.

But against Auburn in the 2010 title game, Oregon had 75 yards rushing and averaged 2.3 yards per carry.

You could argue that Kelly's offense got better and the team wasn't the best offensive one that Oregon had during his time.

Fair enough.

So what happened when Oregon improved? When Kelly got that offense revving at its highest RPM, in 2011, his team finished the year averaging 47 points per game. The Ducks had almost 4,200 yards rushing. This was the pinnacle. This was the jugger-naut to end all juggernauts.

They were putting up these cartoon numbers while, again, pulling starters at the half. The season was a playful romp in a meadow filled with wildflowers, with one exception: the Ducks played LSU at the beginning of that season. In that game, Oregon had 95 yards rushing.

The next day, September 3, 2011, there was an article in the *Portland Oregonian* in which Ken Goe wrote, "LSU didn't just beat Oregon; it beat Oregon up." Both of Oregon's starting running backs, LaMichael James and Kenjon Barner, were knocked out of the game with injuries. DeAnthony Thomas, a freshman at the time, was hit so often and so hard he hobbled off at one point and also fumbled.

Let's put this in a broader perspective. This was a one-time deal for Oregon. But what if the Ducks had to play another one the next week? What if they had to go back to work Sunday and prepare for Florida or Georgia—and not Utah or Arkansas State—the next week with a battered group of running backs? What would Oregon's record be if it had to run that gauntlet every year?

Oregon was doing whatever it wanted to do against any non-SEC team it played. It could have probably increased its offensive numbers by 30 percent if it had played its starters after halftime, and against Auburn and LSU they couldn't break 100 yards rushing.

And by the way, in those games against Auburn and LSU, the elite, vaunted Oregon running game was forced to abandon the run. They literally could not run the ball, and they admitted it by not even trying. So instead of pulling their starting running backs and quarterback to take it easy on the opposition, against these two SEC teams Oregon stopped running *because they simply couldn't run*. This from the best running game in the country.

In a way, our understanding of SEC dominance is similar to our knowledge of the health risks of soda. On a surface level, intuitively, you know it's bad to drink soda. But if you dig a little deeper, you find that it's a tsunami of dental and physical decay. It's an absolute disaster for your body. Drinking one or more soft drinks per day not only increases your risk of obesity by 30 percent, but a twelve-ounce Coke has nearly 40 grams of sugar. The recommended daily intake for women is 22. So, a woman would double her recommended sugar intake with just one soda for lunch.

Similarly, we all know the SEC dominance is thorough. We know the numbers—9-0 in title games, seven straight, routinely crushing the Big 12 in head-to-head matchups.

But wait, there's more.

In February 2013, Dirk Chatelain from the *Omaha World-Herald* wrote a really good article that indicates we haven't seen anything close to the end of this SEC dynasty. In fact, what we've been seeing might be closer to the beginning than the end.

Here's where it gets scary: the Sun Belt is exploding with young football talent. The numbers are mind-boggling. Georgia, with only nine million people in the state, produced over the past five years an average of 115 BCS-level, big-boy Division I recruits. Over that same time span, California—population: thirty-eight million—produced roughly the same amount.

It's absurd. Georgia is in the same ballpark as California, and California has four times the number of people, and California is a talent-rich state for high school football. Chatelain's story also notes that Minnesota, Kansas, Colorado, and Nebraska are all down.

There are Plains states we consider to be eternally fertile in football. Take Oklahoma, where they live and die with football. How does Oklahoma stack up? Five years ago, according to rivals .com, Oklahoma was producing twenty to thirty recruits a year. Two years ago it had sixteen. For the 2013 signing date, just ten.

The gap is widening. The SEC is getting stronger. Depending

on what side you're looking from, it's either a problem that's getting worse or an advantage that's getting better.

But wait, there's more.

When Alabama beat Notre Dame in the BCS title game, it was easy to forget the particulars amid the ritualized slaughter that took place. This great showdown between the revitalized Notre Dame program produced a game that was 35-0 shortly after half-time. Once the game was over and Notre Dame was exposed and everyone was finished with all the bowl games, I wondered what would have happened if Notre Dame had had to play Florida, Ole Miss, or Georgia the week following the blowout loss to Alabama. What if they'd had to play *any* SEC team the following week?

Notre Dame was undefeated in the regular season and reached the national title game, but it would have been an underdog to at least *four* SEC teams. The Irish would have been underdogs to *Ole Miss.* Remember, Ole Miss destroyed Pittsburgh and gave Alabama a real push. Notre Dame should have lost to Pitt and might have lost by 50 to Alabama if Nick Saban hadn't backed it off.

We all know the SEC is better, but when it's placed in context, the dominance is so stark that it's sometimes easy to ignore. And it's not getting any better. This disparity is huge, and it's growing. The Oregons of the world that just roll over people, bury the play-book, and sit their starters—they can't move the ball against the SEC teams.

And that Auburn team that held Oregon to 75 yards rushing? The Tigers weren't even the No. 1 defense that year in the SEC. They were third.

But wait, there's more.

Where is the competition going to come from? Who out there can—pun intended—turn this tide? The Big East is falling apart.

The Big 12 is gasping for air. The Midwest is losing population and recruits.

Where? Who?

The only teams I see with an opportunity to puncture this bubble are either Urban Meyer/Ohio State or USC. Meyer is an extraordinary recruiter and he will dominate what's left of the top-flight Midwest recruits while dropping into the South to poach a few major guys just because of who he is and what Ohio State stands for.

The advantage for USC is this: they don't have to compete against a bunch of college-football monoliths for California recruits. They're one of the few colleges from Denver to the west that is committed and all-in on football. In a good year, USC can get eight to ten of the top players in the state of California. And they can do that every year. Even Alabama is not going to get the top six players in the South—they have to battle everyone else for them.

Yes, coaching is important, but to compete in this new world, recruiting is key. If he survives, I think Lane Kiffin is a good enough recruiter to keep USC going through all the NCAA issues it had. They kept him around because they know the history of college sports: if you have qualms about a coach, at least find one who can recruit. If he leaves, you know he's leaving players behind for the next guy. It's great to have a Bobby Knight type, someone who can coach like crazy but can't recruit, but when he leaves, you've got no players and no Bobby Knight to coach them.

It's the best advice I can give an athletic director: if you're going to fail with a coach, at least fail with one who can recruit.

Either Ohio State or USC could possibly build up an arsenal that has an SEC-level appearance. But if you look through a wide lens, it's daunting. The South has always had a religious zeal for the sport, but this is getting ridiculous. The amount of revenue being raised, the salaries being paid, the championships being won, the talent being produced—it's in danger of getting out of hand.

But wait, there's more.

If you listen closely, you can hear little murmurings of what I would call fear around college football. Meyer was recently quoted as making some statements that could be construed as criticism of other Big Ten coaches for their lack of aggression on the recruiting trail. Meyer is clearly a cutthroat recruiter; his first order of business as Ohio State coach was to flip several recruits from other Big Ten schools, which some coaches suggested violated a gentlemen's agreement between the coaches in the conference. And that's the thing about Meyer: he's coached in the SEC, so he knows recruiting has nothing to do with being a gentleman.

In early February of 2013, Meyer was a guest on a Columbus radio station. He was discussing an upcoming meeting with Big Ten coaches. Here is what he said:

> Our whole conversation needs to be about "How do we recruit?" When you see eleven of the SEC teams are in the top twenty-five, that's something that we need to continue to work on and improve.

Do you hear a little fear, or at least concern, in those words? Can't you hear him saying, "Fellas, help us out a little here?" He's saying they have to get some of those players from the South, or they're never going to catch those guys. He's saying he can't be the only one fighting the fight, or else he's bound to lose it, too. If only Ohio State and Michigan are capable of putting together top ten recruiting classes, those kids are going to start to go somewhere else.

The northern-climate schools used to have it good. Real good. Twenty-five, thirty years ago, the places to play were mostly cold and drizzly: Notre Dame, Penn State. Washington, Nebraska, Ohio State, Michigan. What happened? I'll tell you what happened: ESPN happened.

When ESPN decided to go full-bore into televising college football, the landscape changed. When the network went from televising fifty games to close to five hundred, the kid who wanted to be on television didn't have to go to Penn State and suffer through terribly cold winters. You no longer had to go north to be on television. You could have 74-degree fall days *and* get maximum exposure.

It takes a lot of factors to build this kind of dynasty. And like most dynasties, we either love them or love to hate them. There's no middle ground. Right now, and for the foreseeable future, it's the SEC's world. The rest of college football is just trying to find enough oxygen to survive in it.

It's time to wake up, Rutgers; you can't run your program like Tony Soprano ran the Bada Bing!

Reduction Junction,
Love Your Function

Robert Irvine is a celebrity chef who—like nearly every celebrity chef—owes his fame to television. He has a Food Network show called *Restaurant: Impossible*, where he storms into struggling restaurants and goes commando on their staff and business model in a made-for-TV attempt to resurrect their lagging fortunes.

Irvine brings an acerbic tongue and a successful formula. It starts with three words: Less is more.

Trim the menu. You don't need eight different penne pasta dishes and four different risottos. Figure out what you do best and stick with it.

If only the sports world could figure this out. Can someone please cut back the menu, reduce the noise, pare the fat?

We're catering to an audience of indiscriminate gluttons. We're on a steady diet of more: more broadcasters in the booth, more playoff games, more expansion teams, more bowl games, more teams in March Madness.

If sports were a restaurant, its menu would have five pages of chicken entrees: chicken Marsala, chicken Parmigiana, chicken cacciatore, chicken Milanese. On and on with the chicken dishes.

We've gotten duped into thinking more is better.

More is *not* better. More is simply *more*.

What does *more* do? It dilutes the talent, clutters the landscape, and clouds our opinion of what really matters.

Can someone please give me less? How's that for a revolutionary concept: I want less. Cut it back, reduce it, do whatever you have to do to trim the sports menu.

We need a Robert Irvine for the sports world.

Maybe I'm out of touch. Maybe it's just an unavoidable quirk of the culture. Maybe *more* is inevitable.

Every time I watched coverage of the presidential election on one of the news networks, it would drive me crazy. Twelve different political pundits are jammed onto one set, jostling to get out their sound bites. There's so little time to deliver each message, and nobody has a chance to provide anything remotely resembling depth.

It's gotten the same way in televised sports. If ESPN and the NFL Network add any more people to their draft coverage, it'll be a Broadway musical.

Les Melkiperables.

More, more, more. March Madness, one of our last remaining five-star gems, is on its way to becoming March for Everyone Who Can Beat Virginia Tech on a Good Night.

The tournament is up to sixty-eight teams. That's too many. What makes it even more absurd is that no 16 seed has ever beaten a 1 seed. Four 15s have beaten a 2. Do we really need four more teams that can't be found without a GPS, who play in gyms without baseline seating?

It might get worse. Syracuse coach Jim Boeheim has suggested the NCAA increase the number of teams in March Madness to ninety-six to make for a better tournament.

Hey, I've got a great idea: I think the Four Seasons should drop its room rates to $26 a night to make it a better hotel.

As it stands now, the attendance at first-round games of the tournament is poor, even with the new pool format that allows for teams to stay closer to home. You can trot out the whole "Cinderella" argument to bolster the case for more teams, but that's mostly a smokescreen. Yes, occasionally a VCU or George Mason will make an improbable run to the Final Four. A crazy story like Florida Gulf Coast does happen every once in a while.

But rare exceptions prove one thing: they're rare.

In college football, Louisiana-Monroe once beat Nick Saban's Crimson Tide. Appalachian State once beat Michigan. Should we include those schools, if unbeaten, in BCS bowls? Since when have we changed foundations, budgets, or plans based on rare exceptions? Sixty-eight teams is too many. Ninety-six would be way, way too many.

Why are we so intent on overkill? Tell me this: If there's a power outage, do you immediately go out and buy an $8,000 generator or do you light a candle, open a bottle of wine, and make love to your wife? You mean you can't make it twelve hours without electricity?

That's what a ninety-six-team NCAA Tournament would be: an $8,000 generator for a twelve-hour power outage.

And then there are the bowl games. Don't even get me started on bowl games. We now have a bowl game sponsored by a credit union. You mean a feed store wasn't available? The local tire shop couldn't make it fit in the budget? By the way, do the members of the credit union realize their fees just went up so the third-string safety for the fifth-place Pac 12 team can get a $1,500 swag bag with the newest noise-reduction headphones?

You can't tell me there's a market for some of these lower-tier bowls. Your typical music video has more people in it than you'll find in the stands of some of these bottom-feeder bowls.

Okay, so maybe this doesn't affect you as a sports fan. You don't like bad bowl games, so you don't either attend them or watch them on television. But the overkill in sports—especially pro sports—can't help but impact your life if you're a fan. More teams and more games translate into more average players on rosters and more people like you paying more money for bad products.

I've got a theory on life that applies to this discussion: if you don't have a nickname by 17, you don't need one. Nobody wants to call you Gator or Big Daddy. Similarly, if you didn't have a pro sports franchise by the '70s or '80s, you probably didn't deserve one.

We don't need most of the teams that have arrived since then.

Let's take a look at a few of the most recent franchises introduced in America. I'll just give you a list:

Charlotte Bobcats (2004)
Columbus Bluejackets (2000)
Arizona Diamondbacks (1998)
Tampa Bay Rays (1998)
Vancouver Grizzlies (1995)
Jacksonville Jaguars (1995)
Colorado Rockies (1993)
Miami Marlins (1993)
Orlando Magic (1989)
Charlotte Hornets (1988)

What do most of these franchises have in common? They've struggled from the moment they entered their respective leagues. Some of them had so little support they no longer play in the same city. There was simply no market for them.

But the beast had to be fed. *More* is the only thing that mattered.

The same principle, sadly, seems to apply to the media. Sideline reporters in football and basketball can be valuable; so can pit reporters in NASCAR. The viewers need to know when a fuel valve breaks on Jeff Gordon's car. But three announcers in the booth and two more on the sideline?

Five people? Seriously? It takes only four to perform open-heart surgery.

If you treat your Twitter account like an ad hoc ad for a

modeling agency, then trust me on this one: nobody cares what you say while you're holding a microphone and standing on the sideline at a football game.

The NBA has expanded its first-round playoff series to seven games. Do you need seven games to come to the realization that LeBron and the Heat are better than Brandon Jennings and the Bucks? Apparently, eighty-two games wasn't a big enough sample size.

The NFL is discussing a plan to expand to Europe. You know what, Roger Goodell? This isn't a coffee chain. Lattes play everywhere, but American football doesn't. Nobody in Jacksonville cares about the Jaguars; they're going to be mesmerized by those same Jaguars in Dusseldorf?

In Major League Baseball, Tampa Bay—a talent-rich team with the most entertaining manager in the game—can't draw despite playing in a star-studded division with the Yankees and the Red Sox.

What's the problem in Tampa? If you tell me it's because they need a new stadium, I just might come unglued. Stop with the New Stadium Argument. I'm tired of it. How did that work out for the baseball team—and the citizens—in Miami? That's a fine empty stadium they've got there.

Arguing that a new stadium is going to fix your team is like arguing that a new house is going to save a failing marriage.

There's some basic demographic realities at work here. Not every city in America has the geographic ability to be a port city. Similarly, not every city has the population, affluence, and Fortune 500 support to be a port for a major professional sports team.

Let's get specific: the Tampa Bay Rays, one of those expansion franchises we didn't need in the first place. All it would take is some rudimentary market analysis to tell you the Rays were going to struggle despite being one of the better-run franchises in the sport.

Break it down: 20 percent of the population in the area is over 60 years old; Saint Petersburg has a median family income of $34,000, and 18 percent of the population is below the poverty line; Florida is our most transient state, and many if not most of its baseball fans claim teams from outside the region as their favorite.

Need more? The state of Florida has just sixteen Fortune 500 companies—Tampa has one (WellCare Health Plan), Saint Pete has one (Jabil Circuit). In a sport in which as many as 70 percent of the season tickets are purchased by corporations, that's a big deal.

It's not the stadium; it's the demographics, stupid.

Baseball tried to make the argument that regular-season baseball would work because spring training always worked. Sorry—two different animals. It's easier to get Marge and Hank into their Cadillac on a 75-degree spring day to pay $7 apiece to watch a spring training game when they can park and walk seven steps to the ticket office and eight more to their seats.

It's quite a bit different to get some old boy to park his Delta 88 outside a big-league ballpark, where the cheapest tickets can be four times as much and it's unbearably hot walking a half-mile from his car, another 100 yards to his seats, and 100 yards every time he has to get up and go to the bathroom or hit the concession stand.

In short, let's stop treating sports leagues like Rite Aids and Walgreens. There are a finite number of shortstops—or power forwards—I'm willing to pay to see. Even Vin Scully, the greatest baseball broadcaster ever in many eyes, said on ESPN Radio a few years ago, "Baseball is not only filled with lots of Triple-A players, but right now some Triple-A teams."

Vin is right. Unfortunately, fans don't get to pay Triple-A prices.

Maybe I'm just out of touch.

Maybe it's a futile argument.

Maybe we're just addicted to *more*.

I've found that even when reasonable people make a reasonable argument regarding reducing *anything*, they're treated to harsh criticism. When New York mayor Michael Bloomberg wanted to limit large sodas, he was lampooned in the New York press and met with outrage among a big percentage of the populace. He wasn't asking people to limit the number of children they could have. He was just trying to limit their probability of getting teenage diabetes.

But maybe I'm wrong. Maybe we live in the world of Big Gulps and the New Orleans Pelicans and more Triple-A players in Major League Baseball. But as comedian Dennis Miller once said, "Crap plus crap just equals more crap."

I have restraint, despite what people think. I didn't drink or gamble for sixteen years. That's why I'll never forget my seventeenth birthday.

My Pitch for Pith

One night during my days of living in the Pacific Northwest we had an unusual—and unusually fierce—ice storm. The next morning, I stumbled to the porch to grab the newspaper. It wasn't there, so I expanded my search to the lawn.

No luck.

I was nearly out of hope when I spotted the paper: stuck in a boxwood hedge, one end pointing skyward, the rest of it in a death-grip freeze inside the hedge. Pulling it away was like yanking an ice-cream bar from the hands of my son.

Clearly, the kid who delivered my paper had a poor strikeout-to-walk ratio.

I still wanted to read the paper, so I went to the garage and grabbed some trimmers. I cut the paper from the bush and brought it inside, where I found that the delivery kid was also a lousy wrapper: some of the pages were iced together.

I canceled the paper that morning.

I didn't cancel the paper because I suddenly got dumb or because it was too liberal or because I decided I no longer wanted to be informed about the world outside my house.

I ended my twenty-year relationship with the newspaper because it could no longer figure out how to deliver itself as quickly and smartly as other media. I was growing loyal to information in other forms, and that morning's frozen paper was the tipping point. It was time for us to break up.

It wasn't me; it was them.

My reaction to the errant delivery kid is a small example of a larger point. The media has changed dramatically, and I will say this without qualification: it has changed for the better.

Everything comes at us faster and from more voices and in different forms. Sometimes information even comes at us in 140 characters or less—and that's OK. I'm tired of the bitching about the loss of the old media. The old media voices want us to believe that the new forms of information distribution are making us dumber and less curious.

They decry Short-Attention Span Nation, to which I say: Bullshit.

You want to go back to the good old days, go right ahead. I'm going to try to stay up with the new technology, because I've got news for you: the good old days sucked.

The national IQ is up 4 percent in the last decade, which puts a dent in the argument that we're all getting stupid. If young people are so attention-deprived, why does every mind-blowing technological advance seem to come directly out of the mind of some 28-year-old in Silicon Valley?

You know what I like about the new media landscape? More voices from more places. Yes, I'm a long-time sports media guy with a national radio show and I said that: more voices make for a better media.

More blogs, more media outlets, more athletes with direct access to fans through Facebook and Twitter. I'm all for it. It doesn't reduce my impact. If it means I have to work harder to get and keep your attention, so what? I don't feel threatened by that. I'm willing to take on the challenge.

In the end, you win.

And if you want to counter by telling me there are too many idiots spouting on Twitter, I will agree with you and counter your counter with two words: avoid them.

There's wheat. There's chaff. Figure out the difference and move along.

See? It's not that hard. We have choices, so make them. Ignore people whose opinions aren't worth your time. You are a consumer in a media "store" the same way you are a consumer in a grocery store. If you don't like broccoli, don't put it in your cart. If you're on a diet, avoid the donut aisle. If you don't like crackpots on Twitter, avoid them.

Eventually, it will shake out the way business always does. The marketplace will decide the winners, and they won't be the bottom-feeders. History tells us as much. Tabloid television had its run, but eventually consumers realized it didn't stuff enough meat in the sandwich. Reality television will eventually have to up the ante, too—we won't be amused by singing competitions and odd-ball river people for much longer.

You want to know what networks see as the next big battle-ground? Live sports programming. It's dramatic, passionate, and authentic. It puts the *real* in reality television, and it's winning.

If you're one of those who sits back and grumbles about how much better the media was in the good old days—and it's pre-dominantly older journalists who feel this way—you're siding with nostalgia based on mythology. How good were the good old days? Watch a Walter Cronkite newscast sometime. From limited video to unpolished production values to dull and wordy scripts, it's not what you think it was. Yes, Cronkite was the broadcast journalism god of his time. He was wonderful in a crisis, but just try watching 97 percent of his newscasts.

I dare you.

It's human nature to remember things more fondly after the fact. A University of Illinois professor once did a study on happiness in which he sent roughly a dozen participants on a Florida vacation. For the study, he called them several times a day and asked them to rate their level of happiness from one (something close to a colonoscopy) to ten (ultimate bliss).

When the group returned, he asked them again how much fun they had and asked them to give corresponding "happiness numbers" to the exact times they had previously rated.

Almost without exception, he found that his participants gave much higher numbers after they had returned than they had during the vacation. In other words, they embellished their sense of pleasure as time passed.

Just like the media: folks, the good old days just weren't that good.

Watch a football telecast and compare the information, graphics, camera angles, and production with those of even twenty years ago. Today's work makes an old telecast feel like antique shopping.

Speed is paramount. Sports information is delivered with an urgency that allows the public a more transparent view of how the media works. It can be raw and unpolished, and sometimes it changes even as it's being delivered.

Inevitably, this creates the potential for accuracy to be compromised, one of the leading charges of the old-guard media. We should wait until we have all the facts, they say, rather than running the risk of creating hysteria or damaging reputations with a rush to report.

And I agree—to a point. We should never rationalize or trivialize the importance of accuracy, but the urgent dissemination of critical information has become the top priority.

Would you rather wait to hear about your wife's affair with the neighbor in full detail—with complete accuracy and background information and quotes from four neighbors—or would you prefer to get all the available information *right now*?

If someone leans over your cubicle and shouts, "Drew Brees just got traded to the Cardinals," how deeply do you need the coverage to go? Do you need an intricately detailed account of salary-cap ramifications and conditional draft picks that will never affect either your fantasy team or your life?

No, you got pretty much all you needed from those eight words. That doesn't mean you lack depth or intelligence; it just means you want the most important part of the story, and you want it *now*.

Besides, you can get all the intricate details tomorrow morning in the frozen paper.

Old-media types will tell you that people are less informed in a quick-hit culture. But can't I argue that the fan who doesn't need every detail of every trade might actually be a busier, more productive person with a broader life, a more vibrant career with real family responsibilities who doesn't spend huge chunks of his life crafting lineups from his six fantasy league teams and racking up 17,682 message-board posts under the nickname Bodacious Bammer Benny?

Let me tell you a story. Several years ago ESPN held a contest to find the most knowledgeable sports fans in the country. After all the results were tabulated and the deciding was complete, they were rolled into my radio studio one day for an appearance on my show.

My God, you should have seen these people. They looked like a dozen guys who slept on the floor of a train station while the overnight custodial staff tossed them scraps of food. I asked if any of them were married. None were. In hindsight, it was pointless for me to even ask.

My point—without trying to be too mean—is this: the fans who seek *all* the information, the ones who live and die for the history and the trivia and every Sunday's list of NFL inactives, are not always the freshest bread in the bakery.

Those guys were the outliers, no doubt voracious consumers of the old media. But like any other business, the majority of consumers decide what's important, and right now speed and pith rule the day.

Too many members of the media value their work more than consumers do. Who says your column or four-part series is vital? Interesting and important can be two separate things.

There's long been an argument in journalism: Do we give them what they *want* or what they *need*? The problem with the question is obvious: Who decides? It shouldn't surprise anyone that those who consider journalism a calling are often—you guessed it—journalists. I can think of several professions, from the Peace Corps to law enforcement to teaching to health care to the military and the clergy, that are more inspiring and selfless.

No doubt journalism plays a vital role in our society. That's one of the reasons I decided to pursue it. Keeping an eye on powerful corporations, politicians, and government entities is integral to a strong democracy. Nobody ever said it wasn't, but who ever said we want or need twenty-four inches of news type to dissect a city council meeting or a zoning issue? The inability of newspapers to attract large audiences for paid online content means the information was never as relevant as they might have suspected. Meanwhile, *USA Today*—the ultimate in news pith—is a fixture of the culture.

It should be noted, as many old-media types lament the brevity of modern news dissemination, that NPR—with its depth of thought and witty analysis—is the most listened-to radio network in the country. There are still many long-form, old-school programs thriving on network and cable television. There's *Frontline* and *The*

Charlie Rose Show and *60 Minutes*. Would that be possible in a country full of nitwits?

We've seen an absolute explosion in analysis/opinion pieces. They've gone a long way toward replacing straight news reporting. Everyone has an opinion, and it's the consumer's job to figure out which ones are reliable and educated and which are not. Choose wisely and you get perspective along with your nuts and bolts. Why is that a bad thing?

When my stockbroker informs me of a trend, I simultaneously seek other opinions. I want a broad range of opinions, whether it's from a financial analyst or a barista. I'll figure out which ones are valuable and which aren't. So why can't a reporter, in the midst of reporting a breaking story, be able to voice an opinion on it?

The bottom line: you have been empowered. You have become your own gatekeeper, and this is a threatening development to many in the old media.

You may not always be right, but you're speaking loudly and clearly and with one voice. On the whole, your track record for making the right choice is awfully good.

I trust you, because I'm one of you.

New Orleans is crazy. Every time I fly into Louisiana, there's a layer of fog. I wonder if that's God's way of saying, "I don't even want to know what's going on down there."

The Long Invasion

Failure is such an intrinsic part of the business world that it's almost become a badge of honor. At the very least it's an understood and accepted rest stop on the bumpy and competitive road to success. Nobody hits it out of the park on the first swing—not even the most mythical figures.

Bill Gates's first company was not Microsoft. It was Traf-O-Data, which went Belly-O-Up. Henry David Sanders, aka Colonel Sanders, had his secret recipe rejected 1,009 times, which makes you wonder how it ever remained so damned secret.

Failure becomes just another chapter in the legend, a momentary but necessary battle with adversity that can be used as motivation or instruction to avoid pitfalls in the next venture. There are examples everywhere. Facebook is one of America's most revered companies, but would you believe it owes some of its success to a spectacular failure? Before it became a favorite target of late-night comedians, Myspace.com was a similar social-networking site. Facebook became a staple of society—and Myspace was relegated to the tech dustbin—because it made one simple yet important change to the formula by permitting only designated "friends" to have access to your information. This eliminated Myspace.com's primary weakness and removed the "creeper" factor. Sometimes a revolution is only a slight tweak removed from failure.

This brief history lesson is intended for anybody who might doubt the future of soccer in America. Despite the sport's previous missteps, you will be proven wrong. Really, really wrong—as wrong as those 1,009 doubters who rejected the Colonel.

Soccer is here to stay. Count on it.

How can I be so sure? How can I predict the sustainability

of a sport that so many football-loving, Bud-drinking folks in the heartland consider boring, stupid, and anti-American?

You've heard it before. Soccer's cult leaders have predicted a soccer revolution in this country several times. It was going to happen in the '70s, when youth leagues sprouted and kids by the thousands started chasing the ball around on Saturday mornings.

When I was a kid we were force-fed the idea that Kyle Rote Jr. was America's great soccer hope. This was the best we had to offer? Damn, talk about making it tough to love soccer. No wonder there was such a reflexive backlash against the game.

Rote was nobody's idea of a transcendent figure. He was wooden in all phases of the game—on the pitch and in his personality. He looked like a football player who took up soccer late in life, and he seemed as natural with a ball on his foot as Paris Hilton at a homeless shelter.

Rote didn't make the soccer evangelists lose their religion, though. Every decade brought a new proclamation. It was either the World Cup or Freddy Adu or someone or something else, but The Great Soccer Revolution was always around the corner.

You could be forgiven if, by the fourth or fifth time, you stopped listening.

This time is different, and here's why:

For a sport to occupy a spot in our national psyche, it has to develop a deep connection with its fan base. This can't be done overnight. It can't be done on the backs of one or two great players. It can't be done solely on the power of media attention or the words of the bug-eyed zealots.

It has to strike somewhere beneath the surface for it to connect with people, to get them to invite it in and let it stay awhile. It has to be visceral, and right now we are entering an era where soccer has developed a visceral connection with the American sports fan.

There are four main reasons soccer is carving out a permanent piece of the American sports pie:

1.   **SHARED EXPERIENCE** Fathers and mothers have played, which means kids can have a conversation about soccer on their way to the game, during the game, and afterward. This conversation takes place on a different level than it did in earlier generations, when parents didn't fully understand the game because they hadn't played. Sports are nothing more than emotional connections, and the biggest emotional connection is between kids and their parents.

2.   **INCREASED EXPOSURE** The kid who played a soccer game on Saturday morning can now come home and watch a game on television. This extends the emotional connection.

3.   **VICARIOUS ENJOYMENT** FIFA soccer is a huge hit in the video game world. FIFA '12 was the highest-selling sports video game of all time until FIFA '13 came along and topped it. It was the top seller in forty countries. Kids love this game, and it provides another link in the chain of emotional connection. Through the power of this one video game, like it or not, soccer has become part of everyday life in millions of households.

4.   **GEAR CONQUERING ALL** There is now soccer merchandise. For many kids, wearing a Man U jersey or a Liverpool jersey is as natural as wearing a Red Sox jersey. This is a hugely significant point, because the increase in kids wearing soccer merchandise makes it part of the lifestyle.

These four visceral connections with the sport ensure that it's going to increase in popularity. It's not going to be a capital-*R*

Revolution. It's never going to overtake any of the major sports. And it hasn't exploded on the scene the way the zealots and cult leaders told you it would. Instead, it gradually but persistently wedged itself into the national sports psyche through a series of cultural and sociological shifts.

In the '80, '90s, and 2000s, the experience was limited to playing the sport. Once the game was over, the experience was over.

You'd come home and resume normal programming.

The old soccer experience used to be like going on a date and not talking until the next date. *See you in three weeks.* There was no texting/Twitter/Facebook. Soccer in the '80s was like communications in the '40s: limited and sporadic. You might love it, but it's hard to fall in love with anything if you don't have a deep and consistent connection.

Now soccer is a much bigger part of a deeper and more consistent conversation. How do cultural barriers get knocked down? From the ground up. How does McDonald's make customers for life? Get them hooked on Happy Meals at a young age.

The TV/video game/merchandising is soccer's texting/Twitter/Facebook. It's a revolution in a minor key.

Soccer has forged a gateway into the lives of teenage boys. Young people—and especially American young people—are the most voracious consumers of technology. They've grown up with it, and it has created a certain amount of impatience. *I want it, and I want it now.*

They're the caffeinated generation.

What does soccer provide them? Continuous play, forty-five-minute halves, over in two hours. Baseball is a far bigger commitment: three, three-and-a-half hours.

Soccer's resonance grows with every connection.

I'm not the only one seeing this. When every network is

simultaneously competing for a property, it's a pretty good indication that it's offering something of value. The people making those decisions aren't guessing—they have the demographics and projections on their side, and they're seeing these growing connections. They get it.

Soccer has limitations, no question about it. It lacks that jingoistic quality that we as American sports fans love. We didn't invent it, so it's not woven into our DNA. Soccer isn't *ours* the way football, baseball, and basketball are *ours*. It doesn't have the high school and college connection that make football and basketball feel so uniquely *ours*, or the history of baseball.

Sports fans are like everyone else: protective and provincial and a little bit scared of something that feels like it comes from a different culture. Forty percent of Americans never move more than twenty miles from where they were born. Soccer takes a more open, exploratory mind than most of those people possess.

Remember: I'm not predicting soccer will overtake the NFL. We'll never gamble on Arsenal or the L.A. Galaxy the way we gamble on the Steelers and Cowboys.

But it's here, it's real, and it's not going anywhere.

To me, it's kind of like margaritas: an occasional, and welcome, change of pace. It's not an everyday thing, which means I'm not watching the inferior domestic leagues like the MLS, but the English Premier League or the World Cup? Yes, please. And judging by the ratings of ESPN's World Cup coverage, I'm not alone.

Many of the criticisms of soccer always sounded just a little unfair. They were reflexive rather than well considered. If you didn't know any better, you might even think the critics were making cultural statements rather than athletic ones.

Take the whole "flopping" thing. The red-blooded American sports fan recoils every time he sees some skinny Spanish guy brush past a defender and fall to the ground like he's been tasered by airport security.

Excuse me, but have you watched the NBA in the past decade? That's the same NBA that had to institute a policy of heavy fines for players who flop. It became such an issue in the NBA that the league deemed it a threat to the integrity of the sport. Tough, non-soccer guys like Dwyane Wade and Tyson Chandler throw themselves to the floor with impunity if they're so much as bumped in the late moments of a crucial game. And yet, they're worshipped as heroes while the soccer players are ridiculed.

And, of course, there's never enough scoring or action in soccer. *It's boring.* Somehow soccer is boring but a late-season Padres game—with all the energy of a soybean harvest—is a sacred part of the national pastime? And I hate to break it to every beer-swilling football-and-NASCAR fan, but the average NFL game has somewhere between twelve and sixteen minutes of action, and half of every big NASCAR race seems to roll past on a yellow caution flag. So let's not pretend every minute of every American-made sport is a testosterone-laced beehive of activity.

Here's another thing about soccer: it's got demographics on its side. The "Browning of America" is a huge boon to soccer. The Hispanic population is becoming a larger and larger segment of our population, and soccer is in its cultural bloodstream. Soccer is their NFL.

It kills me when people treat soccer like it's an infestation. We're a country of excess. The Kardashians are okay but soccer is un-American? People get territorial. We can't even call it football like the rest of the world because we have our own football, so that stuff they play with their feet is soccer.

Again, it won't be the NFL, but it's not going anywhere, either.

Over the past few decades, Soccer Guy has stepped away from

the pulpit. He no longer needs to evangelize because he's no longer defensive. He sees the traction his sport has gained and he knows it's not going anywhere anytime soon. He doesn't feel the constant, nagging need to defend his sport.

Anti–Soccer Guy has softened some, too. He sees soccer everywhere—on ESPN, on *Fox Sports*. It's better than he thought, or he doesn't really see it as a threat anymore. It's not taking away his NFL or NBA. He can still watch his Cowboys on Sundays, so he's reached a sort of angle of repose with the whole deal.

And that's where we stand, with soccer making inroads quietly, persistently, and on its own merits. It's not some sleeper cell intent on taking over our God-given right to football, basketball, and baseball. It's a great sport that deserves its spot in the buffet line of sport.

The only major seismic shift left for soccer is the emergence of Soccer Jordan, a transcendent American player who makes even the most hardened Anti–Soccer Guy grudgingly flip on the TV to see what all the fuss is about.

And in a twisted way, one of those all-American sports might unwittingly help soccer move toward that moment. If more and more parents steer their sons away from football because of long-term health concerns, more and more athletes will turn to soccer as an alternative.

That's all right. We can share. There's room for everybody and plenty to go around. And for the first time, that's soccer over there in the corner, ready to make itself comfortable. It might as well pull up a chair and order a drink.

You're not a hero if you put out a fire you start.

For Us, Bias

What I'm about to tell you is not a revelation on the level of Watergate or Clinton-Lewinsky, but it needs to be said: everyone in the media—whether it's politics or business or fashion or sports—has favorites.

It's that word again: *bias*. When it comes to the media, it's gone from being a buzzword to being the worst insult possible. *You're just biased,* people say when they want to discount a story or an opinion they don't like. It's almost too easy.

Well, of course we're biased. Everybody has favorites, and nobody is completely impartial. Do you have a favorite niece or nephew? Do you like one or two of your kid's friends better than the others?

With that out of the way, I admit I've always been more concerned with a different word. This word allows me to overlook your bias.

Access.

Do you have it?

If you have it, I want it.

And the more you have, the more bias I will tolerate.

Former Dallas Cowboy star quarterback Troy Aikman is now a star announcer on Fox. In my opinion, he's the best football analyst in the business today. When I listen to Aikman, I don't hear his bias, but I understand that his current and former employers leave him open to that charge.

No matter what Aikman says, an Eagles or Giants fan is going to interpret it in a certain way—a way that takes into account Aikman's days as a Cowboy and assumes he's a homer. If Aikman says, "Dez Bryant ran the wrong route," a Giants fan hears, "If Dez

Bryant had run the right route, he would have scored easily on the Giants' overrated secondary."

There's nothing Aikman can do to combat this. We all understand he's close to Cowboys owner Jerry Jones and even though he would undoubtedly love to see Jones rewarded with playoff wins, he's also smart enough to refrain from openly rooting for him on the air.

There is something Aikman can provide that few can rival—access to the Cowboys. His history and connections get him behind the rope line. What that means is this: it's my job to decipher his coded messages during his broadcasts with Joe Buck. If Aikman says, "I think some people in the organization could be getting frustrated with Tony Romo," I feel confident I can figure out the rest. Troy had lunch with the Cowboys' owner on Friday or Saturday, and that's exactly what his old boss told him.

Aikman's access more than compensates for any bias—real or perceived—and I'm a more educated viewer because of it.

What I don't want is bias *without* access. Or bias without expertise.

Which is why I've never understood why the sports media have so much damned power when it comes to voting for awards and Halls of Fame.

It's one thing to have strong opinions in a column or on a talk show. Neither of those have much staying power; they're here and gone in an instant in today's 24/7 sports and news tsunami.

Hall of Fame voting falls into a different category altogether. It is tied inextricably to a player's legacy. Seasonal award voting isn't quite as permanent, but bonus structures have created financial implications for players. These votes help shape and forge legacies and commerce. In the case of the Hall of Fame, the voting creates the closest thing we have to sports immortality.

To put it bluntly, I want the right people with the right access controlling those votes. The media can be included—in certain situations—but we need to stop treating the media as the overwhelming and often exclusive authorities on such matters.

It works in other industries. In movies, nearly six thousand people vote on the Oscars, 22 percent of them actual actors. The other votes are cast by directors, producers, animators, composers, executives . . . you get the idea? Highly qualified people.

People behind the rope.

Do these people have agendas? No question.

Do they have access and insight? Absolutely.

In music, the Grammys are chosen from the votes of 150 experts from various musical fields. Artists, producers, engineers . . . you know, people with access. Voters can vote only in their area of expertise, which means a jazz artist can't vote on Best Gospel Album. The Rock and Roll Hall of Fame's nomination committee has six hundred members including artists, historians, and working industry veterans.

You can almost hear Garth from *Wayne's World* saying, "Who would know rock better than those who rock themselves?"

I'm not anti-sportswriter. And God knows I'm not anti–talking head. But listen to the numbers on some of these sports panels:

The NFL Hall of Fame, the shrine of pro football immortality, bases its inductions on the opinions of thirty-seven people—all of them media members.

How many could diagram even one play? If they were all in a room, how many would be able to tell the difference between "Z right wiggle, 24 fox chase, double tight left, zap set on two," and "tight right, eagle slant and go, 44 jet Zebra motion and set"?

How many have watched any film at all? How many go to training camp every summer? Don't you think an eleven-year NFL player like Archie Manning would have a better sense of greatness than, say, a columnist who was promoted from beat reporter and doesn't even cover practice with any regularity?

And yet people like the columnist—and not people like Manning—are the arbiters of football immortality.

The voting for the Heisman is so regionally biased that it borders on embarrassing. Andrew Luck, the best college quarterback I've ever seen either live or on television, claimed only a third-place vote on one ballot in the South, where perhaps they mistook Andrew Luck for a magician or a scratch-off game.

Who got the first-place vote? A running back from Alabama, of course, who ran behind an offensive line filled with future NFL high picks and gained an impressive 1,600 yards. But a closer look reveals that four of his five biggest rushing games were against North Texas, Georgia Southern, a two-win Mississippi team, and an Auburn team that was 1-5 against ranked teams.

In the 2012 Heisman race, Johnny Manziel won five of six regions, and deservedly so. Where did he lose? In the Midwest, where voters went with a linebacker, Notre Dame's Manti Te'o.

Manziel produced over 5,000 yards of total offense and forty-seven touchdowns in college football's best defensive conference and almost single-handedly turned his program around by beating No. 1 Alabama on the road.

Te'o, whose popularity was based partly on Notre Dame mythology and partly on Dead Girlfriend mythology, had fewer tackles as a senior than he did as a junior. And not only that, but in November, as Notre Dame was pursuing an undefeated season with some of its biggest games, Te'o had just thirteen solo tackles in four games.

The NBA got into the act in the 2012–13 season—media voters were woefully off-target when they voted Marc Gasol as NBA

Defensive Player of the Year. The thirty NBA head coaches—you know, the guys who study film and organize game plans and see every player in the league live and in-person—didn't have Gasol on the All-NBA first-team defense. To take it a step further, the coaches didn't even have Gasol as the best defensive player on his own team. That honor went to guard Tony Allen. To make matters worse, it was the second straight year the media's number one pick didn't merit first-team accolades from the coaches.

These are the same voters who bestowed upon Phil Jackson just one Coach of the Year award despite his eleven NBA titles. That means Jackson has won as many awards—one—as beleaguered Lakers coach Mike D'Antoni, whose teams have such a reputation for poor defense that he's called Mike Antoni. (Drop the *D*—get it?)

Sam Mitchell has a Coach of the Year plaque in his trophy room, too. It came in his lone winning season. His career record? 156-189. It would be hysterical if it wasn't so regrettable.

And baseball . . . baseball might be the worst.

You have to be a member of the Baseball Writers' Association of America for ten years to vote for the Hall of Fame. The problem: many of the members who have a vote don't cover the sport regularly. Some don't cover it at all. A writer who covers a team for a year can remain a dues-paying BBWAA member even if he immediately leaves the beat after that one year and becomes a food writer.

According to Tyler Kepner of the *New York Times,* some writers still voting have spent decades with no involvement in the sport whatsoever. Baseball's voting structure means that our hypothetical food writer has a vote but Vin Scully, the most eloquent and informed baseball broadcaster ever, has no vote.

Eleven voters kept Babe Ruth from being a unanimous first-ballot Hall of Famer.

The Sultan of . . . say *what*?

Bias seeps into everything. It's part of the human condition, so instead of raging against something that's inherent in all of us, learn to filter it and manage it. Think of it as accepting the flaws in your mate. The love flows more easily when you aren't searching for—or demanding—perfection on a daily basis. You understand the flaws and appreciate the gifts.

Halls of fame and awards in sports shouldn't be controlled by people who lack a behind-the-rope quality. They can be part of it—jury—but not judge. Once I filter out the bias, I need to form an opinion based on what's left.

So stop fixating on bias and concern yourself with access and insight. If you can take me places I can't see or experience without you, that's a special relationship.

But if you don't think Babe Ruth is a first-ballot Hall of Famer, or if you can't see that Phil Jackson is substantially better than Sam Mitchell, I'm going to be left with no choice but to reduce your power to influence anyone's thinking.

But your bias? Forget it. I'm already over it.

My parents or teachers often relied on proverbs or maxims in times of crises. They were the guiding lights through chaotic times. At least that was the intention. Most were really corny but a handful stand the test of time.

"Do unto others as you would have them do unto you" is a pretty solid message in any era.

The one I struggled to get my arms around was always, "You're only as strong as your weakest link."

At least in sports, that's just not always true.

During the Michael Jordan era, considered the NBA's golden age, the bottom of the league was atrocious. While the Bulls were piling up 72 wins in 82 regular season games—seven other teams had fewer than 30 wins. Yet television networks have no obligation to broadcast bad teams. The NBA should use this motto: "We are as strong as our strongest are."

Television revenue has far surpassed gate revenue for most sports leagues. Owners and leagues flourish when they sign multiple lucrative network deals. Those deals don't have stipulations handcuffing networks to lousy teams. No network ever has to broadcast a Jacksonville Jaguars game. In essence, deals are all about your strongest and most interesting, not your weakest and least captivating, teams.

Salary caps have mostly eliminated dynasties in professional sports. Great teams are disassembled due to financial restraints. Furthermore, you can only afford so many stars on one team, which even limits how good the very best can be. Even the best teams have holes now. Everybody has weaknesses. It's mostly about having the talent that can make plays or change the direction of a close game. With added scouting and technology, nobody can hide their flaws.

It's no longer about your weakest link as much as it is about having a top end or a transcendent star nobody can defend or stop.

The Miami Heat are maybe the worst rebounding team in the NBA in a league that habitually rewards that. They have been to three straight NBA Finals because nobody has figured out how to slow down LeBron James consistently.

A hot goalie can erase all sorts of flaws for a hockey team. Find him and sign him.

A few years ago the Connecticut Huskies won a national title while only finishing tenth in the Big East during the regular season. You don't finish tenth without several weaknesses. How did they do it? Nobody could stop guard Kemba Walker once the tournament rolled around.

Get great at something and spend less time trying to fix every little problem. You can win with weakness.

For the record, I still think you should treat others the way you wish to be treated.

Guys are consumed with being right, instead of getting it right.

A False Positive

You know what America really needs? Another Tim Tebow column.

At this point, roughly seven years into our bizarre national obsession with the world's most famous backup quarterback, there's nothing I can serve up that you haven't chewed, swallowed, and digested a hundred times. So I've decided to take a different approach by discussing the word *sustainability*.

You know the word. It's trendy, a buzzword with chefs who seek seafood either caught or farmed in ways that take into account the impact on the long-term vitality of the oceans. It's a buzzword in the construction industry, where a more enlightened approach has caused builders to use processes and resources that are more environmentally responsible.

From food to floors, people are seeking sustainability.

An NFL franchise is no different. Every general manager and player-personnel guy should be building his team with sustainability in mind. You look at *now*, sure, but you look at now with an eye on tomorrow. You've got to build something that not only lasts but doesn't destroy all your future resources.

This is where Tebow comes in.

Damn it, Colin, you said this wasn't a Tebow column.

Sorry. I bluffed. But stick with me. This will be the most valuable Tebow column ever written. There's a lesson to be learned for all mankind here, I promise.

Of all the fashionable words of our time—*fusion, fiscal cliff, web-friendly, pesto*—*sustainability* is the king. So why not link it with something we all love?

No, not Tebow.

Football.

The foundation of every pro-Tebow argument consists of two words and two words only: *he wins*.

That's the homing beacon, the shining light in rough waters, pointing them toward safety.

For the record, he's won eight, lost six, and split two play-off games. Statistically, he does win more than he loses—by two games. I'm willing to let the Tebowers have this one, though, because even the most ardent among them don't claim he's Peyton Manning.

Tebow's problem in the NFL is more intrinsic to his style. His way of winning is not viewed as sustainable by the league's sharpest minds. His quarterback ratings in his sixteen NFL starts read like interstate highways: 32, 88, 20, 38.

That's not a six-lane highway to the Super Bowl.

If you want to win big and win regularly, your quarterbacks not only have to be consistent. They also have to be consistently good.

The average QBR of the last ten Super Bowl–winning quarterbacks is 93.3.

Tebow's career average: 75.

That's not close.

We're not comparing Picasso to Matisse here. We're comparing Josh Groban to a $50-a-gig wedding singer. For coaches, a 75 QBR gets you fired.

And consider the context. Tebow's abysmal 75 rating is taking place amid a new, pass-happy, spread-offense world, with repeated rule changes that favor receivers. Nobody can regularly stop a good passing offense in the NFL these days, but Tebow can.

All by himself.

This isn't a *scheme* or a *fit* thing. It's not as if Tebow just hasn't found the right organization to maximize a unique skill set. When

the Patriots shocked the football world by signing him—for no
guaranteed money, I might add—the first question anybody could
ask was what position he would play under Bill Belichick. What
does that tell you?

All coaches and general managers are chasing the same white
whale: a franchise quarterback they can build around for more
than a decade. Does that seem like a grandiose plan? Maybe, but
take a look at the top fifteen quarterbacks of all time based on
passing yards: Joe Montana, Tom Brady, Drew Brees, Peyton Manning, Dan Marino, John Elway, Brett Favre, Johnny Unitas, Terry
Bradshaw, Dan Fouts, Fran Tarkenton, Troy Aikman, Bart Starr,
Roger Staubach, and Warren Moon.

You see where they're going with this? The average career
length of those fifteen quarterbacks is 14.8 years. Three of them—
Manning, Brees, and Brady—have years left. Staubach brings the
average down slightly; he played only eleven years because of his
military commitment. Moon started his career in the Canadian
Football League and didn't throw a pass in the NFL until he was 28.

The average career of those fifteen quarterbacks is more than
four times longer than the average starting career of a college
quarterback. This is precisely where the debate over Tebow—the
crux of the *he wins* confusion—lies.

Tebow was perfect in Gainesville. But college football is transient. Almost everyone—players and coaches alike—are using their
current job as a stepping-stone to something bigger and better and
higher paying. Players leave after a couple of years, assistants want
to be coordinators, coordinators want to be head coaches, and
head coaches want to be head coaches at bigger programs or the
NFL. Unlike past generations of head coaches, the Schembechlers
and Hayeses, even the top college coaches bolt. Urban Meyer got
sick, literally, and left Florida. Pete Carroll fled USC so fast he left

a contrail. Nick Saban absolutely loved LSU, until all of a sudden he didn't.

The dynamics are different in the NFL. There are no stepping-stone jobs—the league is the final step. There are thirty-two of those jobs in the entire world. If you win, even in a spectacularly unglamorous place like Buffalo, you stay forever or until you get booted.

Some jobs don't have an upgrade. In television, it's the unwritten rule of the late-night talk-show host. You get that job, you keep it and hang on until retirement. It's Mount Rushmore.

The college world is the coaching version of a three-day camping trip to a state park. Whatever keeps you warm for the night is fine. You survive today before you worry about tomorrow. Next week or next year might as well be a different lifetime. Everybody is playing the game within the game, angling for career advancement, determined to do one thing: win *now*.

Sustainability doesn't have the same currency in college football as it does in the NFL.

The only long-termers in college are the boosters. They'll still be here complaining and giving twenty-dollar handshakes forever. But college football has no pension plan for assistants and the players don't get paid, so the sooner they can leave, the better. College is a resume builder—no more, no less.

Pro football can be transient, but not necessarily by design. It's similar to a mortgage, where longevity is rewarded with equity. The quick flip can reduce earning power. Longevity—sustainability, to stick with the theme—allows a coach to build a system that can sustain bad defenses, injuries, tough scheduling, free-agent misses, and bonehead drafts. All of this is predicated on building around a star quarterback who can overcome little defensive support and injured teammates by winning shootouts.

Coaches and players have pensions in the NFL, so once you land the top quarterback it's a signal to tell the wife and kids, "Let's put our name on the mailbox. We're going to be here for a while."

The single-bullet theory espoused by Tebow supporters—*he wins*—isn't always the primary objective in the NFL. It might be hard for the ardent Tebowites to wrap their minds around, but it's true. When Buffalo gave Ryan Fitzpatrick a contract extension on the basis of a four-game winning streak, the Bills were rightfully mocked. When Mike Shanahan allowed Robert Griffin III to play hurt, he was rightfully criticized. Those weren't wise long-term decisions. Every individual win comes with too high of a cost if it derails the larger plan.

The way in which Tebow wins is not a viable option for long-term success. He's a guy who wins low-scoring games by the slimmest margins, with single-digit completions and a sub-fifty quarterback rating every other Sunday.

He is the quarterback version of a battery-powered flashlight: bright at first, increasingly dimmer as it's used, and eventually discarded.

So when fans want to preach the gospel of *Tim Tebow: Winner*, they're thumbing their noses at sustainability and ignoring the bigger picture of the NFL: it's not about winning *this* Sunday.

It's about winning every Sunday for 14.8 years.

In 2013, an NFL team without a good quarterback is like a stripper without a good body.

Nature vs. Nurture

Respected baseball broadcaster Marty Brennaman called the idea nothing short of a travesty. Phillies closer Jonathan Papelbon called it stupid.

What had Cuban defector-turned-overnight-lightning-rod Yasiel Puig done? In sports, the words *travesty* and *stupid* are generally reserved for serious offenses. For instance: crimes against humanity or the game. Maybe defacing property or cheating a teammate. In this case, though, Puig's "crime" didn't reach Al Bundy status, much less Al Capone.

The harsh words and hostility toward the 22-year-old Dodger outfielder stems from this: he had miraculously compiled the best first month of a career in modern-day history. As a result, he was being considered for a spot in the 2013 All Star Game.

That's it.

No punch line here.

In the end, Puig lost out to Atlanta's Freddie Freeman in the fan vote for the final spot on the National League roster. But the reaction from people in the sport—even Puig's own manager, Don Mattingly, said Puig didn't belong in the game—spoke volumes about baseball's inflexibility and crankiness when faced with anything new and fresh.

It's a three-pronged attack: push back, roll your eyes, and publicly mock.

The NBA and NFL embrace new faces. MLB interrogates theirs.

However, instead of condemning baseball, is it possible that we've sidestepped a very obvious explanation? Wouldn't it make perfect sense for anyone who lives in the ten-year cultural tunnel

that produces major-league players to share the same rigid sensi-
bilities?

The answer is that simple: they're a by-product of a narrow
culture.

Baseball players aren't bad people. Tony Gwynn is probably
my favorite *person*—not athlete, but person—in all the years I've
spent in sports. But in general, baseball players are some of the
most difficult and brittle athletes I've come across. They're different from guys in other sports. They exist in an insular world that
revolves around a series of individual battles, and it's inevitable that
some of that will seep into the personalities of its players.

Look at the trends. Domestically, baseball is becoming less
and less of a high school sport. There are very few successful
urban initiatives in baseball. The best players in this country are
being produced by travel baseball programs, where parents and
kids travel all over the country to play game after game in front of
scouts and college coaches and other parents. It's expensive, and
it's a closed society. Nobody outside of it cares about it, or even
knows it's happening. Kids used to play ball with other kids in their
neighborhood, but now a growing number of them play on teams
that draw players from a huge region. There's very little camaraderie in that world, since every parent and every kid is chasing either
a scholarship or a spot in the major-league draft. They're always
looking over their shoulders wondering who's watching them and
who's gaining on them. Some of the fiercest competition comes
from within the team.

As this system has flourished, it's no surprise that baseball in
the United States has become a wealthy, white suburban sport. It's
women's soccer in spikes.

Nearly every kid in this country follows the same path: from
travel baseball to either college baseball or the minor leagues.

College baseball is almost uniformly white, a direct extension of the suburban travel-ball programs. Minor league baseball is as insular a world as exists in professional sports. Players hang out together, but they hang with their own kind. White American players hang out together, Latin players hang out together, Asian players hang out together.

In the major leagues, nothing really changes. It's very cliquey in a big league clubhouse. There are language barriers, so some of the cliqueishness is understandable. But there's also something inherent in the nature of the game that tends to create a certain type of personality: a series of individual battles.

Players are given remarkable freedom once they've established where they fit into the hierarchy. It would be outrageous—utterly unthinkable—for a manager to ask Josh Hamilton to bunt. Hamilton is a power hitter, and power hitters don't bunt regardless of the situation. It could be the most obvious bunting situation, a spot where bunting is by far the smartest option to help the team, and it still wouldn't happen. Same holds true for Albert Pujols, Adam Dunn, Miguel Cabrera, Robinson Cano. It's simply out of the question.

It's a year-round sport, which makes it extremely difficult for professional players to further their education. They go from year-round travel baseball in high school to year-round minor-league baseball, where they're around only other baseball players, to major-league baseball, where it's a clique-y sport centered on individual battles.

What's the opposite of this? Take a look at football. The recruiting is done through the high schools. There is no such thing as travel football for high school kids. High school football is often the most galvanizing element of a high school community. The student body, cheerleaders, band—it's truly a communal event. The competition is team vs. team, city vs. city, region vs. region. There's a huge amount of collective pride involved. Football players are a part of that greater community, and they are more likely to play another sport than baseball players who have devoted themselves to a year-round, singular pursuit.

Football is not the year-round sport baseball has become, which puts football players into contact with more people—parents, coaches, teammates—with different interests and personalities. When they get to college, football players once again become part of a diverse student body. Their games, once again, are communal. Pride in your school—something greater than you—is often a bigger deal than it was in high school.

And look at education: by rule, football players have to take classes for a minimum of three years. Even if they're not scholars, they're still exposed to renowned professors and supersmart peers and levels of thought they wouldn't have achieved on their own. Even in the biggest football factory they're receiving some semblance of an education. They're not just playing Xbox in an apartment in some podunk minor-league town with guys who come from the same upper-middle-class suburban background and play a sport whose schedule makes it nearly impossible to further an education in the off-season.

An NFL locker room is home to a high percentage of college graduates. A professional football player is, in general, more worldly and media savvy and well rounded than a major-league baseball player. It's not necessarily a criticism; these are simply characteristics that are bred into the culture of the respective sports.

As of 2012, just 4.3 percent of baseball's nine hundred major-leaguers had a college degree. It's the lowest of any major sport, and it absolutely has to have an impact on the people who play the game.

There are differences intrinsic to the game as well. Football is not an individual sport. It's a choreographed sport. Snap counts, audibles—I depend on *you* for my *safety* on a set of specific rules based on teamwork. Think about that: it's an awesome responsibility.

Unlike baseball, where it's outrageous to take the bat out of the hands of Pujols, football is filled with situations where the individual is suppressed for the sake of the team. Peyton Manning, arguably the best quarterback of a generation, is told at the end of the divisional playoff game against Baltimore in 2012, *You will take a knee and not throw a pass.*

What does the football paradigm create? Humility.

Let's compare the two:

Baseball is played by suburban and rural young men who are less educated, living in an insular world, driven by individual battles. The insularity of that world is obvious every time an outsider attempts to gain access. Unless you played baseball or cover it for a living, the "outsider" is treated like an alien. There is very little patience for the newcomer. Oh, and one other thing: once a player gets to the big leagues, his contract is guaranteed. There's a certain level of invincibility that comes with that kind of security.

Football, on the other hand, is played by young men who are from all walks—suburban, rural, urban. It's not insular; it's broad based. They come up being part of a campus, a member of a diverse and open community. They play a choreographed sport based on efficiency and teamwork. Their contracts are not guaranteed, and they can be cut at any time.

As a football player, you have less freedom. You have an assignment, and your job is to do your assignment and your assignment only. You are scolded if you go out of your lane or miss an assignment. Despite the stereotype of the football player as a big, muscle-bound aggressive beast, I find football players very easy to deal with. They're humbled constantly. Their careers are cut short by injuries all the time; the threat is like the sword of Damocles hanging over their every move.

It seems counterintuitive to suggest that athletes whose careers depend on violence are the more civil species, especially in light of the Aaron Hernandez situation. However, I find people whose livelihoods are associated with violence—from football players to police officers to paratroopers—tend to be more humble. They need other people for their safety, and that one sentence—*I depend on you*—is strong medicine.

Nothing against baseball players—they just don't exist in the same hypercharged environment. Their world is more insulated and bound by tradition and custom. They can't help themselves; they're made that way.

Former LSU star
Honey Badger is
a paradox.
Great football
instincts yet dreadful
life instincts.
Maybe he should
just wear a
uniform all day.

Luck, Meet Genius

Take a look at the biggest guy in the room. He's about 6 foot 5 inches and 240, which gives off an intimidating scent. But does big always equal tough? For all we know, he could have just inherited really good DNA from his large, muscular Norwegian father. He could be deathly afraid of carpenter ants. He could bawl his eyes out at Celine Dion concerts. He could have less courage than your average senator. You see his size as an advantage in life. He could see it as a curse.

Which is another way of saying this: sometimes you get the benefit of the doubt in life, even when you don't deserve it.

It just so happens that I have something in common with the biggest guy in the room. In my case, the perceived advantage concerns sports gambling. I don't know where my aura comes from, but it's there. Maybe it's because I lived in Las Vegas for seven years. Maybe it's because I once rubbed out a guy who gave me lousy information on a Lions game. Or maybe it's because I set some sort of world record for correctly picking NFL games in 2012. Whatever the case, there are some people out there who think I really know my stuff.

The truth is . . . no, wait. Let me back up for a minute. The *partial* truth is that I was pretty freaking amazing with my NFL picks last year. However, the larger truth is this: beyond me being amazing, there was some blind luck involved.

I have some advantages. I have a little better access to former players and coaches than you do. I might get a slight edge by using tidbits of information gleaned organically throughout the week, scouring some free scouting report services offered by ESPN and other media outlets, and monitoring a handful of different betting services. I also bet without an ounce of emotion or loyalty. So yeah—those factors might provide an edge.

A slight edge. *Slight* as in "I'm slightly better than your cousin Larry 'The Velvet Touch' Lassaro but probably not as good as Larry's good friend, Tony 'The Golden Retirement Plan' Valdosetti."

Here's all you need to know about betting on professional football games: if you asked the actual head coaches, the guys who have built game plans all week and slaved over game tape with their assistants, they'd tell you they couldn't and wouldn't regularly pick winners against the spread. How do I know this? Easy—I've paid attention to the former coaches who broadcast games. They watch tape all the time. They get inside juice from their buddies who are still coaching.

And these guys—these smart guys who know the game and have inside information—couldn't pick out drapes to match a couch.

It is nothing more than educated guesswork. Any wise guy will tell you it's *when* you bet that helps you make the profit. The real sharps bet games as early as Monday morning when the lines are usually posted first. That should tell you one thing: if you're waiting until Friday for my picks—or the picks of some radio goober—you've already missed the best lines of the week. You can't get the freshest produce if you're shopping four days after it's been delivered.

The real pros also bet several times on the same game as a means of protecting their slim annual profits. Fans can fail to fully understand the nature of the game. You're betting against odds-makers' lines. In other words, you're betting against professionals who sit in a room and say, "Let's create a number to bet against for this game that makes it virtually impossible to make a living predicting who wins."

Yes, Pundit Tracker—a website that follows media picks—named me the most accurate forecaster for politics or sports in 2012.

And yes, two weeks into 2013—based on the same polling—I trailed stray cats on *Animal Planet*.

Occasionally fans ask me if I bet my own picks. That never makes any sense to me. Why would you care?

Would I only use a respected doctor to save my daughter's life if and only if he'd saved his own daughter with the same procedure?

Can I never use a marriage counselor who's had troubles in his own marriage? Does a bankruptcy attorney merit respect only if he, too, had to file for bankruptcy? Must a dermatologist have perfect skin?

Advice comes from all over. If you feel it's quality information, use it. Even the so-called mavens in the world of sports gambling have off-weeks and even down years. Billy Walters, profiled on *60 Minutes* and recognized as the industry's sharpest and wealthiest bettor, was not having a particularly memorable 2012 with his NFL picks.

Me? Well, that was a different story. After hitting my eighth or ninth straight winning week, I got a call from a well-connected friend of mine in Los Angeles. He wanted to know if he could get my picks early. When I asked why, he said, "Billy's guys told me they may just follow your lead for the next few weeks. You're the hottest guy in the country."

That's one way to look at it, I suppose. Here's another: I was probably just the luckiest.

There's a reason Wall Street and prisons are filled with men. We manage money better than we manage ourselves.

Home Alone

Cesar Geronimo was buried near the bottom of the star-studded batting order of the Big Red Machine of the 1970s. Slender but strong, an elegant outfielder with a respected arm, he probably wouldn't have even made the team without his defense. He had a nonchalant style, gliding more than running, and occasionally he'd wear an old-style batting helmet without an earflap. He had speed but never seemed to steal as many bases as he should have.

Everybody knew Pete Rose and Johnny Bench, but insight on Geronimo could set you apart from other kids.

One day Geronimo was behind in the count to Dodgers lefty Doug Rau, himself an overlooked guy on a roster of bigger names. The count was probably 1-2, and Geronimo put a big, swooping swing on a fastball—low and away, if I remember correctly—and pulled it over the short set of trees for a home run.

In my front yard.

I was twelve years old and coming to the realization that I was alone. All the time. Maybe this memory is embedded in my brain because Geronimo had only 51 career homers and I had finally come to understand how desperate I had become in my efforts to entertain myself.

My sister, Marlene, five years older, left junior high and high school about the time I was entering both. We shared precisely zero friends and, really, what fourteen-year-old girl wants to hang with a nine-year-old brother? She had her Beatles and Peter Frampton albums, and I had my imagination.

I didn't just talk to myself. I talked back—even argued.

My early years were probably no different than many of yours, especially if you, like me, came from a small town. In rural areas, convincing your mom to drive you across town is the difference between riding bicycles and laughing all afternoon with a friend and playing a doubleheader in your front yard.

Alone.

And entirely in your head.

My mom once drove over my whiffle bat. It ended the season. It was June.

That was a *long* summer.

I'm not pleading for sympathy or suggesting I'm a victim of bad parenting. Instead, I would like to spend a few minutes defending the isolated. In fact, I'll take it a step further: I'd like to declare myself the official spokesman for the solitary.

Loneliness is misunderstood. For me, isolation has always been a thought-provoking partner.

I've spent large chunks of my youth in it. It took me a while, but I eventually came to understand what a valuable friend it is. Friendship often works that way—it grows on you over time.

I define people and groups of people with one word: noise. I explain it to those who come from a different background by saying, "I prefer quiet." It sounds like a confession, but it isn't.

I speak for millions; we're out there, and we're okay.

Trust me, we really are.

We seek the out-of-the-way nooks in life, corners that most people never see or view as lonely outposts. To me, *alone* is not an epithet.

Don't get me wrong. I don't always prefer to be alone. There are plenty of times when I could use a friend. I was driving home, alone, from a USC-Syracuse football game in New Jersey once. The game went long because of a stoppage for a tornado, never a good sign. Driving home, the roads were wet and covered with leaves. There was a power outage in one town, and my lonely SUV provided the only available light on one abandoned road. That felt flat-out lonely, and not in a good way. I needed to hear another human's voice, but after several cell phone calls went unanswered, I think I called my accountant for an update on the tax ramifications of something or other. Come to think of it, it may have been someone else's accountant. At the time, I didn't really care.

For the most part, though, unless it's my immediate family, alone wins.

I worry about the future of reflection and quiet contemplation. Will social media applications like Twitter and Facebook serve to eliminate even occasional self-examination—alone time, silence, even forty-five minutes of doing nothing more than asking yourself questions that only you can answer? It's vital for personal improvement, even personal maintenance. But is it destined to go the way of the dinosaur?

And no, you can't have a retweet on your birthday. Sorry, but being born isn't original and concentrating on something unimportant is a tacit reminder that you haven't put in the time to make any of us think, least of all yourself. When I look at all the minutiae that gets mistaken for something important—look, a photo of my food!—it seems we've replaced self-reflection with self-obsession.

Here's a novel idea: spend less time trying to get popular and be noticed. Spend more time creating something that will not only get you noticed but will be substantial enough to make people stick around and watch. You know what that takes? Alone time, that's what.

I'm not here to condemn collaboration, or the ever-popular concept of the group discussion. Bouncing ideas off people has considerable merit.

But in this nonelection year, I would like to campaign for the solitary pursuits. Jogging. A long drive without a blaring radio. Hitting golf balls. Staring out of an airplane window. Sitting on a deck and watching a distant lightning storm. Those—not crowded rooms or smart phones—are the breeding grounds for my ideas.

The question I'm asked most often about my radio career is a fairly predictable one:

How do you talk to yourself for three hours a day?

What I want to say in response is this:

You should hear the other fourteen.

I'm okay with it. Really. So is Cesar Geronimo. At least he should be. After all, he got credit for a home run he never hit.

ESPN is similar to a big hospital. Journalists are the heart surgeons and talk-show hosts are just the plastic surgeons.

Swing and a Miss, and
a Miss, and a Miss

say this without reservation or fear of contradiction: nobody likes to be wrong.

For our purposes, let's stay away from the garden-variety miscalculations. We're not talking about missteps like, "Damn, I left my keys at the Donohues'." This is the big stuff. *Big* as in Julia Roberts marrying Lyle Lovett. *Big* as in there's absolutely nothing in Al Capone's vault. *Big* as in Evel Knievel jumping over a canyon.

These are hideous mistakes, horrendous lapses in judgment, blunders so horribly off-base that the only recourse is to stop on the side of the interstate and revel in the glory of the steaming tire fire you created.

In other words, to *own* it.

It seems much harder for guys to do this. We're raised to be leaders, to be dependable, to be logical and rock-solid providers for our families. They count on us. But *wrong*—pathetically, irretrievably wrong—is tough to admit. It translates into undependable, misinformed, and unreliable. Damn it, that's not who we are.

After all, we're the ones who wrote the United States Constitution. Never mind that it's been amended twenty-seven times since, and we've even amended one of our amendments. I'm on a roll here. We are men. We need to be right.

I've been wrong. I'm not too proud to admit it. I've been really, really wrong. I'm about to own a few of these times publicly and ingloriously to my shame and for your amusement. But first let me attempt to explain my wrongness, to place it into the proper context so I can make *wrong* sound as right as possible. Hey, what can I say? I'm a guy.

Through the years there have been very few people in the media I consider so talented or informative that I can't miss what they have to offer. There just aren't many people who give me a unique, can't-find-anywhere-else narrative that pulls me in every time.

Andy Rooney's pieces on *60 Minutes* were like flypaper for me. Jon Stewart's opening twelve-minute rants on *The Daily Show* have the same adhesive quality. Former *New York Times* op-ed columnist Frank Rich is in the same category.

It might have taken me a while to excavate my way to Rich's columns in the Sunday *Times*—the thing's roughly the size of the San Antonio phone book—but I never missed one. His takes on the mass media and politics seized my attention for the quality of the writing, and always made me think. He took angles where others took shots.

In his final column before departing to *New York* magazine, Rich delicately described the anguish of the opinion-maker. "The routine can push you to have stronger opinions than you actually have."

Truer words have never been lamented.

But where Rich had a once-a-week column, I have a once-a-segment obligation to summon a strong opinion. If you make a habit of issuing weak, I-can-go-either-way opinions on the biggest stories, the radio ratings system, called PPM, will punish you into oblivion. Sometimes it feels like a Three Stooges skit, when stories are breaking in real-time and you're being fed information in one ear and throwing out your perspective almost simultaneously. In our short-attention-span culture, listeners give you no more than twenty seconds, on average, to make a point or they're gone. There they go—Radio Runaways.

And that's why keeping one eye on the scoreboard can drive you crazy. You're going to swing and miss. You're going to be looking for the fastball, get the changeup, and look completely foolish as you lunge and miss and fall down in the box. It's inevitable.

I'm more Olive Garden than prix-fixe French restaurant to begin with, so filling time and space—and lots of it—is a job requirement. I don't have the luxury of a copy editor, and I can't let my opinions marinate for twenty-four hours before the white smoke billows from the chimney and I deliver my royal decree.

Hell, no—I've got to talk, and talk *now*.

Now, back to me being brutally wrong.

In my two decades in sports radio, two or three whiffs stand out.

I thought—no, check that, I *knew*, deep in my bones—that Ryan Leaf would be a better NFL quarterback than Peyton Manning. This wasn't even a tough choice. Manning had nervous feet. He was immobile. His body looked like it was molded out of Brie. In his biggest college games, he wore a deer-in-the-headlights look that spelled disaster against bigger, faster, meaner NFL players. He had NFL-caliber talent surrounding him at Tennessee, especially at the skill positions, and yet this character couldn't beat his rival. Ever.

However, Leaf . . . Leaf was a different story. Big, strong, fearless, he stood in the pocket looking downfield for his undersized, undertalented receivers as the defenders rolled off him. He threw darts to guys whose skill sets would be mocked by CFL general managers. Leaf was confident, bordering on cocky. He was a man among boys. Manning was anxious and often overwhelmed.

Good lord, this opinion produced some significant seismic activity on the sports Richter scale.

Peyton Manning, it was later discovered, is actually Deep Blue, the chess computer that beat Garry Kasparov. Manning = Deep Blue, if computers threw pinpoint crossing routes. He's mechanically and intellectually the perfect QB life-form. And Leaf? Well,

Leaf dissolved into a life-form that resembles circa 1980s Sam Kinison on a bender.

There's no reason for me to stop here. When it was reported that Kevin Durant was unable to bench-press 185 pounds in the days leading up to the 2007 draft, I went to town on this information. I buried Durant for days. I didn't only criticize the kid; I mocked him. I unleashed my vitriol in a condescending tone; I wasn't sure he'd have the strength to dress himself before games.

I kept at it, even after a long-time scout assured me the kid was for real. He was built like a breadstick, but he had the kind of range nuclear submarines envy. Yeah, whatever. What does an expert with twenty-seven years in the business know?

I'm not exactly sure what happened to Durant, although it's been reported in some circles—probably alternative newspapers with minuscule circulations and irresponsible writers—that he's actually turned into a decent . . . ah, fuck it: Kevin Durant is amazing, and I was dead wrong.

In no particular order, I hereby present to you a sampling of a few other tiny, slight, relatively incorrect predictions I made on the air. I'll even use the actual quotes from the broadcasts, just so you don't miss out on any of the subtleties and nuances I brought to these could-go-either-way opinions.

PREDICTION/GUARANTEE: "Mike Tyson's trainer could beat Buster Douglas."

WHAT ACTUALLY HAPPENED: Not *precisely* that.

PREDICTION/GUARANTEE: "Tom Brady and Randy Moss can cash their Super Bowl–winning checks now. The New York Giants are overmatched."

WHAT ACTUALLY HAPPENED: The checks bounced.

PREDICTION/GUARANTEE: "Notre Dame is done playing
for national titles. Fifty-year-olds still think they're
relevant. Not recruits."

WHAT ACTUALLY HAPPENED: I'm still not entirely sure. How
did they go unbeaten again?

PREDICTION/GUARANTEE: "The 2013 NCAA Tourney will
be different. Take underdogs, not favorites. This is
the year of the little guy."

WHAT ACTUALLY HAPPENED: The exact opposite.

In closing, that felt really good. Cathartic, almost therapeutic.
There's a weight off my shoulders now. There's no reason to bottle
up that kind of angst and let it fester inside you. Just let it out, give
it some air, see where it goes.

Being defensive serves no purpose. As a therapist once told
me, the faster you own your own baggage, the faster you can create something new. It's an opportunity to take more risks, to live
boldly, free of the fear of being wrong.

By the way, did I ever tell you how right I was about Tim
Tebow?

Acknowledgments

What is luck, and how do you define it?

Do we create our own or is it truly random, landing in our laps without discretion or reason?

It was drilled into me from an early age, probably from coaches, that accomplishment followed a direct path, beginning with setting a goal and working hard to achieve it. That equation leaves little room for good fortune or bad breaks. You control everything, and reliance on anything or anybody is simply a weakness, right? It invalidates all that hard work you pour into something. Over time, though, I've come to understand that we all need some luck. Occasionally, we all land some.

And if not for a healthy dose of it, this project would have never been completed.

After spending two years writing columns, ideas, notes, and one-liners on everything from napkins to legal pads to an airsickness bag, I was frustrated. My schedule was crammed with a radio and television show that left me exhausted at the end of every week. One night on my deck, drinking wine and lamenting the process, my wife, Ann, gave me an ultimatum: finish the book or stop complaining about it. Either way, I needed to control my destiny. For a woman who doesn't enjoy much about sports, she became a great coach that night.

From that point forward, the pieces started to fall into place. Good fortune played a key role.

In a random conversation with ESPN's Matthew Berry, I was connected to literary agent Richard Abate. After struggling to connect with two previous book agents, I drove to New York almost resigned to the inevitable conclusion of the project. Instead, his instincts and energy were a perfect match.

We agreed that in order for this book to come together I needed to work with a sharp and experienced writer who would push me—and the project—to a new level. "Have you heard of Tim Keown? He cowrote that book you were just reading in my office. I'll give him a call."

Tim has several bestsellers to his credit, and I drove home that night figuring my chances of landing him were somewhere, statistically, below slim. But people do occasionally hit holes in one. A man once landed a jetliner on the Hudson River. It could happen, right? College tuition isn't getting any cheaper. Maybe he has several kids. Hopefully thirteen.

A few days later I was told Tim had agreed to help me.

There is no other way to put this—good fortune was on my side that day.

Many people say that writing books is a daunting and exhausting experience. It wasn't easy, but I've never enjoyed any project or teammate more in twenty-five years in the business.

I viewed each of our phone calls as an opportunity to prove to Tim that he wasn't wasting his time. That's how respect works, at least for me.

I feel lucky to have worked with Tim and I just want him to know that. I want you to know that, too.

About the Author

COLIN COWHERD is currently the host of *The Herd with Colin Cowherd* on ESPN Radio and ESPNU. He is also a former cohost of the show *SportsNation* on ESPN2.